TAX TARGET: WASHINGTON

TAX TARGET: WASHINGTON

Gary Allen

Introduction by
Howard Jarvis

'76 PRESS

Seal Beach, California

Published by
'76 Press
P.O. Box 2686
Seal Beach, Calif. 90740

First printing, Paperback, 100,000 January 1979
Second printing, Hardbound, 25,000 March 1979

International Standard Book Number 0-89245-016-9
Library of Congress Catalog Card Number 79-50458

MANUFACTURED IN THE UNITED STATES OF AMERICA

Contents

Dedication

To my children, and yours, in the hope that they will see Americans recapture our heritage of limited government; that they will be able to keep the fruits of their own labors; and that their labors will build a freer, more prosperous nation for us all.

Acknowledgements

My highest regards and deepest thanks to Howard Jarvis, for proving that an informed citizenry *can* build a pen around the bureaucratic hogs; to Robert Welch, for keeping the battleground lit with a beacon proclaiming, "lower taxes through less government";

To Mike Culbert and Chip Wood, for the hours of effort that went into converting a bulky manuscript into a finished book;

To Evelyn Davis and Kitty Koepping, for the clipping and copying, the typing and correcting, that helped produce a manuscript in the first place;

To all of the "toilers in the vineyard," whose efforts to stop Big Government from enslaving us all have made the coming victory possible.

Introduction

When I began my campaign fifteen years ago for Proposition 13—property tax reduction *by law* — not too many people believed it could be done.

The politicians, the free-spending bureaucrats, the layers and layers of entrenched public workers in California barely noticed us. Most of them stifled a yawn, poured another cup of coffee, and went right on doing what they did best: taxing us into the poorhouse.

Even many folks who wanted tax relief—who needed it desperately, to keep a roof over their heads and food in their stomachs—weren't convinced it would ever happen. But they knew they had to try.

Thousands upon thousands of them distributed petitions, collected signatures, sent us the few dollars they could scrape together. Steadily, gradually, then faster and faster, the momentum grew.

By the time they were done, alarmed and angry taxpayers in California had collected over 1.5 million signatures on our petitions. The major hurdle had been cleared: Proposition 13 would be on the ballot in June 1978. Every tax-paying Californian would have a chance to vote on it.

Suddenly, the big-spenders noticed us. They opened wide their war chests and financed a million-dollar campaign against Proposition 13. Every government employee, every teacher, every policeman, every fireman, every city clerk was told his job would go out the window if Proposition 13 passed.

It was all a bunch of barnyard compost, of course. And the people knew it. On election day, June 6, 1978, over four million Californians—two voters out of every three—said, "I've had enough. *Stop taxing me to death!*"

Proposition 13 put the brakes on taxes in California. It made a reduction in property taxes mandatory, by Constitutional Amendment. The people finally had a chance to speak, and their message was heard in every town, every village, every city in this country—from Sacramento, California to Washington, D.C.

We've won a major battle, but not the war. Now, it's time to take on the most wasteful taxocrats in history: the spendaholics in Washington.

In the following pages, Gary Allen confirms your worst fears about how your tax dollars are wasted by the bloated bureaucracy on the Potomac. He shows you how billions and billions of dollars, taken from you by government, go down the federal drain every year.

Tax Target: Washington is a book every American needs to read. It will make your blood boil. But isn't it about time you got angry at what's being done, in your name and with your money?

I urge you to read every word of every chapter in this book. Get your friends and neighbors to read it, too!

Then, demand a halt. If the politicians won't change the policies, then it's time to change the politicians! Only you can do it. And I urge you to start now.

November 1978

HOWARD JARVIS
Los Angeles, California

Chapter One
The Washington Spendathon

Americans are becoming fed up with inflation, taxes, and the mounting encroachment of Big Brother in their lives. The nation's illicit love affair with Big Government is evaporating faster than water on an Arabian sidewalk after a spring shower. One measurement is the discovery by a pollster that the public now has a higher regard for garbage collectors than for politicians. Imagine how Joe and Jane Citizen would rate bureaucrats!

Lou Harris, who does polls for many candidates, has said, "Public aversion to big government has now reached flood-tide proportions. When asked what was the 'biggest threat to the country,' 10 percent of the public selected 'big business,' 15 percent 'big labor,' 32 percent 'big government,' and 32 percent volunteered 'all three.'"

A majority of Americans—over 75 percent—feels that "the trouble with government is that the elected officials have lost control over the bureaucrats, who really run things." The number who believe this, says Harris, has risen eleven points over the past three years. Harris found that 62 percent of the American people believe that the trouble with most "Liberal" Americans is that they think problems can be solved by throwing money at them, and that is dead wrong. An even larger majority, 81 percent, feels that "the trouble with your getting special benefits and hand-outs from the government these days is that you will have to pay for them four or five times over in higher taxes." Sound like you? And, by a seventy-seven to fourteen margin, the public feels that "a candidate who says he can give the unemployed government jobs and not increase federal spending just isn't being honest."

Even though much of the anti-government rhetoric coming from candidates each election year is about as sincere as the pretty speeches of a shipboard Don Juan, Americans should take heart from the fact that even some former worshippers at the altar of Big Government are awakening to the ravages of the bureaucratic Frankenstein. One of the most eloquent flip-flops we have read in recent months was by Phil Tracy in the radical chic *Village Voice* for April 19, 1976. Consider:

> *This story grew from the feeling that nothing in Washington functions any longer .... That the means of government have gradually replaced the ends. That Washington no longer carries on in order to serve the rest of the country but now exists primarily to serve itself.... Nobody, particularly liberals, any longer believes that the policies they advocate or the programs they propose will accomplish much more than the hiring of more government bureaucrats. They don't believe their own solutions....*

Tracy points out that Washington is all but drowning in information. "But there is very little knowledge. And no wisdom whatsoever.... Are the farmers in the Midwest angry? A hearing will be held. A bill drawn. Hire some of their people to do a big study for the Ag Department."

The charades go on, but the people are beginning to

realize that *government* has no real solutions. That it is, in fact, a large part of the problem!

Even more encouraging than the succinct analysis Tracy brings to his dissection of Washington is his approach to solving the problems created by Washington. He actually believes that we must again begin relying on *individuals* to solve the problems we face! Listen:

> *You see, the dirty little secret Washington is hiding from us is that we can't pay people to be compassionate for us. We either do it ourselves, as individuals, or we don't do it at all.*

You can bet that, if even the *Village Voice* has gotten the message we have been sending, it will not be long until that message is fully understood in Washington. In the long war which government has been waging on its own citizens, Americans are beginning to fight back. And it's high time, isn't it? Let's look at just what our tax-mad bureaucrats have given us.

Perhaps the best barometer of gargantuan government is the explosion of government spending. The proverbial drunken sailor on a binge seems like Scrooge when compared to the Washington bureaucracy. The $125 billion spent ten years ago by the federal government was at the time properly considered enormous, but it sure seems puny when contrasted to current budget extravaganzas. Spending this year will go sailing past the half-trillion mark—with about as much fanfare as another Elizabeth Taylor wedding. This is a jump of nearly $50 billion over last year! It is obvious that the bureaucrats in Washington believe the sky is the limit. It is also obvious that if this mad spendathon is not stopped—and soon—the politicians in Washington will bankrupt us, or have us swimming in baskets full of paper money that won't buy a Big Mac with fries.

In the federal swimming pool, billions of dollars are tossed around like so many drops of water. But let's take a look at what a billion dollars really is. It is an amount so astronomical that it almost seems meaningless. In our dreams we can picture ourselves as millionaires. But a billion dollars—a thousand million— is simply a mind blower. (It doesn't seem to mean much to the politicians in Washington either!)

Consider: One billion seconds ago, the first atomic bomb had not exploded; one billion minutes ago, Jesus was still on earth. Or, to put it in a monetary perspective, if you spent one million dollars at the rate of $1,000 a day, it would take two years and nine months to spend it all. But at $1,000 a day, it would take 2,739 years to exhaust one billion dollars. Now, our government manages to blow almost $1.5 billion every day, rain or shine, including Sundays, holidays, and the day of the Super Bowl game.

The budget used to increase by a billion or two every year; then it escalated to an increase of five billion dollars per year; then ten billion, twenty billion, thirty, and now *fifty billion dollars* a year.

It took 174 years—from 1788 to 1962—to reach outlays of one hundred billion dollars by our federal government. It took only nine years to add the second hundred billion dollars. And just four years to pile on the third. Now we are adding a hundred billion in just the Fiscal 1977 and 1978 Budgets. If this is not stopped we will be adding seventy-five billion dollars a year to federal spending within a year or two, and within four or five years we will pile on one hundred billion in a single year.

The federal budget is so out of control that it grows by leaps and bounds whether there is a Democrat or Republican in the White House. All our Presidents pay lip service to controlling spending. Even Lyndon Johnson, the man who was so poor he had to borrow his fare to Washington (and then retired after years of government service with a fortune conservatively estimated at $14 million), once proclaimed: "We must tighten our belts; we must adopt an austere program." It turned out to be austerity for us, not for the politicians buying votes with our dollars.

The spending madness seemed to horrify candidate Richard Nixon. He denounced it as reckless, even called it "dangerous fiscal madness." Campaigner Nixon promised us tax-burdened serfs: "I say it's time to quit pouring billions of dollars into programs that have failed...."

When Richard Nixon wrested the Presidency from the Democrats in 1968, federal spending, hyped by the "guns and butter" programs during the height of the Vietnam War, was $183 billion. After eight years of Elephantiasis, spending in Washington had exploded to a gargantuan $423 billion. That's $240 billion in eight years, or an *average* increase of $30 billion a year.

Of course it is standard Republican procedure, especially in fund-raising letters to the party faithful (and gullible), to blame all of this increase on the "Democrat-controlled Congress." This is not without a large grain of truth. But, when the G.O.P. finally gets into the White House, it often tries to outdo the Democrats in coming up with "creative," "progressive" solutions to problems.

The Department of Health, Education and Welfare was born under Ike, and all those wonderful new agencies like the Consumer Product Safety Commission, the

Occupational Safety and Health Administration, the Environmental Protection Agency, and the Federal Energy Administration were born or matured under Nixon and Ford.

What political hullabaloo there has been over federal spending has amounted to a demagogue's delight. When the Republicans are out of office, they wail like banshees over "wasteful government spending." When it is one of their boys sitting grandly in the Oval Office, scores of billions are added to yesterday's bloated, wasteful budget to make it this year's bare-bones budget.

When the Democrats sit in the White House, there is usually no hypocritical palaver about cutting the budget. They talk about "stimulating the economy" and "getting things moving again." And off we go into the wild blue yonder of budget-busting spending programs.

The rhetorical game goes something like this: The Republicans would like to keep the increase in spending down to forty billion dollars or so per year. The Democrats say it must be pumped up by sixty billion dollars. The Democrats denounce the Republicans as heartless skinflints, while the G.O.P. responds with charges of reckless financial madness. Occasionally it may even be necessary for the President to veto a congressional spending appropriation to maintain the facade. "Victory" for both sides means holding the increase at fifty billion dollars instead of sixty.

Every year we fight the Battle of the Budget. And every year the budget wins.

There are three primary frauds used as rationalizations to explain why the federal budget is out of control. The number one rationalization for ever-escalating budgets is that they are now largely "uncontrollable."

In "Budget In Brief" for the 1979 Fiscal Year, it is reported that the so-called "uncontrollables" comprise about seventy-five percent of proposed non-defense outlays. In his State of the Union message, President Carter said that nearly ninety percent of the increase he was proposing over Fiscal 1978 was "unavoidable under existing law."

Why does the budget escalate inexorably every year? Obviously the Congress each year passes new spending appropriations. But there is a more insidious mechanism for inflating the budget. Every year those who are aghast at spiralling expenditures are coolly informed that a significant amount of the increase is "uncontrollable." From where do these "uncontrollable" increases come?

Let us assume that one morning a United States Senator rises in the great hall of the upper house and pleads the case of homeless dogs. Hardly an eye is left dry as the Senator demands that every True Liberal rally to the cause of hobo Bowzers, Blackies, Rovers, and Spots. The cost of federal Canine Care, he explains, will be a paltry one billion dollars... the first year. The Senators say to themselves, well, it's a worthy cause and one billion dollars is a small enough sum when considered against what it cost to put a dog into orbit. So why not? Thus a new spending bill is passed. But, the hooker is that while the price tag the first year is (a nominal) one billion dollars, the Canine Care Bill, like most other legislation, contains a built-in escalator for subsequent years. The cost the second year is three billion dollars, and eight billion the third year, and so on until dogs are running away from home to live lavishly in the federal kennel.

Now, everybody is happy except the bewildered taxpayer, who does not understand how he has been bamboozled. The Legislative Branch, which passed the bill because of the "comparatively low" first-year appropriation, now wraps itself in the pure, white garb of the do-gooder ... and then it ducks. In succeeding years the Executive Branch can claim that *it* is submitting a bare-bones Budget, but that there are many increases in appropriations (now including Canine Care) which are mandated by law.

In a study of the growth of so-called "uncontrollable" federal expenditures, Nancy Teeters, a senior specialist in budget economics at the Library of Congress, says "although these programs are called uncontrollable, all programs are controllable if legislation to change their nature is enacted." Obviously! If any President or any Congress really wanted to control the "uncontrollables," the solution is simple: Introduce legislation to repeal escalator features of laws passed by previous Congresses. How many times has *your* Congressman done that this year?

As long as the public is led to believe that it is impossible to stop increases in spending because they are "uncontrollable," federal spending will continue to soar like a helium-filled balloon. This is nonsense. These welfare laws were not written in stone by the fiery finger of Jehovah, they were created and passed by politicians anxious to buy votes. Spending could be brought under control if Congress had the courage to go back, amend the laws, and stop the open-ended escalation. But less than ten percent of our Congressmen and Senators favor such a course. Most expect to stay in office by providing ever-expanding bread and circuses.

The second fraud used to justify yearly increases in federal spending is that it stimulates the economy and produces increased prosperity. Common sense tells us that this is poppycock. If federal spending brought prosperity to the economy, we would all be flying our own Lear jets by now. Common sense also tells us that taking money away from taxpayer A to give to special interest B does not create anything. It just transfers wealth from politically impotent A to politically influential B. It's called robbing Peter to pay off Paul. Money is drained from people who would spend it on new homes, cars, education for their children, medical care, or a thousand other things. They will also save or invest some of their money—which means it is then invested to create new jobs. When the government takes the money, chances are it is wasted. Certainly it will not be spent as desired by the person who earned it.

For many years, England has attempted to spend itself into prosperity. It has been such a disastrous flop that even some who have championed such activities now see the error of their ways. James Callaghan, socialist Prime Minister of Britain, recently stated:

We used to think that you could just spend your way out of a recession and increase employment by cutting taxes and boosting government spending. I tell you in all candor that that option no longer exists and that insofar as it ever did exist, it worked by injecting inflation into the economy. And each time that happened, the average level of unemployment has risen. Higher inflation followed by higher unemployment. That is the history of the last 20 years. And each time we did this the twin evils of unemployment and inflation have hit hardest those least able to stand them—our own people, the poor, the old and the sick.

He almost sounds like Howard Jarvis, doesn't he? Listen to what else he said:

*You know that we have not been creating suffi-
cient new wealth as fast as we have been distribu-
ting it. It is from a healthy and expanding manufac-
turing industry that we shall be able in due course
to resume the growth and improvement of our social
services and also create the jobs which are necessary if we are to reach our employment targets.*

The spendocrat Congressmen who try to hide their
records from the angry folks back home claim that the
fault for ever-rising federal budgets is with defense
spending. This argument is not only foolhardy, it is
false. The principal justification for the existence of
government is to protect its citizens from aggression. If
our government cannot protect and defend us, then all
debates about what role government may be permitted
in society are meaningless. National defense now takes
only twenty-nine percent of the federal budget. "Social
services" take fifty-eight percent—exactly double that
amount. Each year national defense has been de-
creased as a percentage of the budget and the Gross
National Product. Meanwhile, the socialist slush fund
of the Department of Health, Education and Welfare
was raised a staggering 21.4 percent in 1975 alone.
In 1952, we spent 13.5 percent of our GNP for defense. Since 1959, the level of defense spending has
fallen from 8.9 percent of the GNP to 5.9 percent. Other
federal spending, meanwhile, ballooned dramatically
from 11.6 percent to 16 percent of the GNP. If you listen
to "Liberals," you might think that millions of Americans go barefoot and die of starvation because our resources are being poured into the gluttonous maw of
the mighty military-industrial complex. Actually, only
5.3 percent of our labor force is involved in defense
work—down from eight percent a decade ago. The

military now uses only three percent of the goods and services of the economy—half that used ten years ago.

It is not the defense spending segment of the budget which has exploded. It is the social welfare portion. Keep in mind, defense is the principal reason for the existence of government. Our Founding Fathers in the Constitution tried to prevent the creation of a government whose chief activity was to rob hard-working Peters to give the money to politically influential Pauls. But today, robbing Peter to pay Paul programs are our number one spending items.

These are called "transfer payments." Transfer payments to persons are defined by the Bureau of Economic Analysis as "income payments to persons, generally in monetary form, for which they do not render current service." According to the *U.S. News & World Report* of November 28, 1977, last year these transfer payments from Washington totalled an incredible $249 billion—double what we are spending on defense. The newsweekly added, "the income-support payments account for 53 cents of every dollar the Government spends. This spending represents a five-year increase of 106 percent, or an increase of over 20 percent per year."

These transfer payments from workers to nonworkers represents 17 percent of all personal income. At least 55 million people are sharing the booty! The big four welfare programs which have made enormous jumps in the past five years are Medicaid (115%), Aid to Families with Dependent Children (60%), Food Stamps (184%), and Supplemental Security Income (179%). The news magazine informs us that there are 178 additional federal programs involved in transferring income to those who did not earn it. It adds: "Person for person, direct and indirect payments equaled $1,150 per American in 1977, compared with $582 in 1972."

Which translates into $1,150 per person in taxes, or $4,600 for a typical family of four.

Most of these programs are under the jurisdiction of HEW, the infamous Department of Health, Education and Welfare. HEW started out spending a mere $5.4 billion back in 1954, and this fiscal year will spend over $180 billion with no end in sight. This represents a jump of $25 billion over last year. And next year's jump will be tens of billions more.

The very astute Senator Jesse Helms is one of many Americans concerned about all of this. He pointed out recently on the Senate floor that "there are now 72.5 million Americans supported by some kind of government program.... Who ends up footing the bill for all this? The obvious answer: The 71.9 million Americans who are currently employed by the private sector." In other words, said Senator Helms, "more people are riding the wagon than pulling it."

The tough Tarheel Senator added, "It is going to get worse as long as we in Congress continue to vote for more programs that cost more tax dollars and make more Americans beholden to the federal government, and not their own initiative, for livelihood."

This is why it is so difficult to cut back government spending. Every program has its own constituency. The recipients scream like wounded Banshees when their own handout is threatened. The collectivists in government have been very clever. They have created a slot at the trough for almost 72 million people. The politicians know that while people resent handouts to others, they fear losing their own. That's human nature, don't you know. So it is much easier to stop a program before it becomes law than to stop it once it has a constituency hooked on receiving government (taxpayer-financed) checks from the Santa Clauses in Washington.

This political fact of life allows a clever politician to go around during his campaign making all kinds of loud noises about economy in government, while at the same time making all kinds of promises to special-interest groups. Generalized opposition to Big Government does not mean much when it comes to specific issues. As Colorado Senator Gary Hart puts it: "Every Colorado delegation that comes to see me has two messages—one, cut government spending; two, get more federal money for our interest." Most politicians don't object to doling out dollars to special-interest groups because every recipient of a federal goodie is not only a potential vote at the ballot box, but a potential financial contributor. And campaign contributions, as the old political pros like to say, are the mother's milk of politics.

This is the politicians' side of the federal spending coin. The other side is that of the recipients, the beneficiaries of federal giveaway policies. Don't get the impression that government's robbing Peter to pay Paul policies are welfare recipients, deserving or not. There are also many welfare programs for the rich and for giant corporations who want to forego the rigors of competition. These very special special interests don't get a $123.50 Social Security check from the government. They get millions of dollars worth of fat government contracts, subsidies, protective tariffs, or special legislation penalizing competitors.

The flaw in our political system, writes economist William F. Rickenbacker, is that it permits special interests to gain private benefits at the expense of the taxpayer. Rickenbacker observes:

This comes about because of the lobbying pressures that are exerted against legislators. A special-interest group knows very well how much it stands to gain from a new law or program in its favor, and it will campaign hard for it, spending time in the legislature's corridors, buying lunches for lawmakers, contributing to their campaign funds, paying for political announcements on television and in the papers, making it seem there's a vast public enthusiasm for the new project.

But where's the opposition? This new project will have to be paid for. Why don't the taxpayers as a group make a similar effort to stop the lawmakers from transferring money from the taxpayers' pockets into the pockets of the special-interest group?

Rickenbacker then answers his own question:

Because the taxpayers as a group can hardly feel it. The $600 million maritime subsidy, for example, costs only a couple of pennies a day for the general taxpayer, all hundred million of us. But it means about $15,000 a year to each member of the special-interest maritime groups! So a few thousand members of the maritime trades can actually put a hundred million taxpayers over the barrel and shake the money out of them. Each individual taxpayer feels that a given program may cost only a few dollars a year, to him personally, and so it's not worth his time or money to fight against it.

And so, piecemeal, program by program, the special interests gain at the expense of the public interest, and the size of government, of spending, of taxes, grows and grows. The taxpayers as a group almost never have the chance to vote on the total size of government spending.

So, some politicians smilingly surrender to the arm twisting by special interests, while others do so grudgingly. The latter know that they are helping to carry the country along the road to bankruptcy, but rationalize they can do no good for the country if they can't get re-elected. After all, as they say in the cloak rooms, losers don't legislate. If prostitution is the world's oldest profession, being a politician has to be the second oldest.

According to the Tax Foundation, a non-profit research group, spending by all levels of government is multiplying like rabbits. Total government spending for fiscal 1977 was $715.7 billion, which worked out to $9,607 for each of the nation's 74.5 million households. This was an eleven-percent increase over fiscal 1976.

In 1960, government spent $151.3 billion, or $2,865 for each household. In fifteen years, therefore, per-family spending more than tripled. During the same period, prices doubled, so spending by government is growing half again as fast as the Consumer Price Index.

This raises the question: Have our democratic systems built within them the seeds of their own destruction? Are we intent on proving true historian Alexis de Tocqueville's doleful conclusion of 200 years ago?

> *A democracy cannot exist as a permanent form of government. It can only exist until the voters discover that they can vote themselves largess from the public treasury. From that moment on, the majority always votes for the candidate promising the most benefits from the public treasury, with the result that a democracy collapses over loose fiscal policy ... always followed by a dictatorship.*

Think about that logic. Isn't that exactly what is happening? Every organization and special interest group is organized to rip off the taxpayer. We have socialism for the poor and socialism for the rich, all paid for by the broad, unorganized middle class. Not only does the middle class not have lobbies and trade associations putting pressure on Congressmen for them, most people have no idea how their own Congressman votes. This allows Congressmen to preach fiscal sanity at home and vote just the opposite in Washington. An observation by a federal judge more than one hundred years ago seems even more true today: "No man's life, liberty or property are safe while the Legislature is in session."

Where are we headed from here if we keep sending the same kind of legislators to Washington as we have been?

You see, this scenario is not new. It has all happened before. No, not in America, because our Founding Fathers built protections into the Constitution to prevent it. But, one by one, those protections have given way to the demand for more and more government services, which produce more and more government spending. The spendathon madness has happened many times in Europe. One of the most recent is Germany of the early '20s. That one resulted in Hitler coming to power in the wake of economic chaos. The same policies being pursued by our government today wound up destroying the Roman Empire. There, a republic was replaced by the rule of the Caesars.

Wait a minute. It *has* happened in America. Remember when New York City almost went belly-up in 1973, after years of runaway spending? Uncle Sam stepped in and bailed out the Gotham spendthrifts. When our federal government follows Fun City into bankruptcy, who will bail us out?

CHAPTER 2
The Tax Man Cometh

It may shock you to be told that Washington's monumental spending spree has to be paid for. But this economic fact of life is as certain as the tide—and as inevitable as taxes. There are three, *and only three,* ways in which the government can finance its spending. The government must either tax for the money, borrow it, or print it. There are no other alternatives. In this chapter we will look just at the tax situation. The other two forms of covering federal squandering will be discussed in subsequent chapters.

Nobody likes taxes. I don't, and I'm sure you don't. It's only a politician who has been described as a person who never met a tax he didn't hike. Practically everybody thinks he pays too much. The truth is that if the average American had any conception of how much he *really* pays, there would be a revolt against Big Brother that would have the majority of our Congressmen seeking new jobs—and hundreds of thousands of bureaucrats clogging the unemployment lines.

It was, of course, a politician who defined taxation as the art of plucking a goose to secure the maximum amount of feathers with the mimimum amount of squawking. And make no mistake about it, Mr. and Mrs. Taxpayer, it is you who are being plucked.

Little wonder that a recent Gallup Poll indicates that a majority of Americans believe they are being taxed to the breaking point. Finally, a nearly naked goose is beginning to squawk.

The most accurate way to compute the total tax

burden is probably to consider government spending as a percentage of total individual income. According to Wesley Hillendahl, director of Business Research for the Bank of Hawaii: "Following the Great Depression, when combined government spending rose to between 20 and 23 percent of personal income, World War II briefly required a level of government spending amounting to more than 62 percent of personal income, accompanied by acute inflation of prices. By 1947, government spending returned to about 23 percent. Subsequently, over the years, government spending has gradually taken an increasing share of personal income. Spending reached 35.8 percent in 1960, and 41.8 percent in 1970. Presently, government absorbs 43.5 percent of personal income, twice the share of 40 years ago."

Right now you are probably saying to yourself that you are not in a 40-percent tax bracket. If you are typical, you are paying around 20 percent in income taxes. But those are just the *direct* taxes you pay. Mr. Average American does not realize that most of the taxes he pays are hidden in the cost of goods and services.

Commentator Paul Harvey puts it this way: "Only *people* pay taxes." His point is that while demagogues and the economically ignorant scream for ever more and more taxes to be paid by giant corporations, the truth is that all such taxes are passed on to consumers in the prices charged.

Another five billion dollars in taxes on the steel industry, for example, means an additional five billion dollars passed on in higher prices to the myriad of industries that use steel in the manufacture of their products. These industries, in turn, pass on the increase to you, the consumer.

Did you know, for example, that the price of a loaf of bread contains 151 separate, hidden, indirect taxes? When you buy bread you are paying a part of the combined taxes of the farmer, the miller, the trucker, the baker, and the supermarket. Obviously these people all have to recover the taxes they must pay, and they do so in the prices they charge for their goods and services. If they could not pass along these costs to you, they would sooner or later go out of business.

There are 100 taxes on an egg! 116 taxes on a man's suit! 150 taxes on a woman's hat! 600 taxes on a house! Even a quart of milk has 87 taxes on it! These taxes accumulate like compound interest, with each additional tax added to each preceding tax. You absorb every single one of them when, as a consumer, you buy the finished product. Up to half the price you pay for a new car, a dozen eggs, or any other product may be nothing more than the taxes already added to it by others, for government.

To look at it another way: If it were not for these direct and indirect taxes, the oil companies could sell us gasoline at just over twenty cents a gallon and still make a profit. *Government* is the reason gasoline costs seventy cents at the pump. *U.S. News & World Report* confirms that personal income tax....

> *is not a full measure of the impact that taxes have on the family budget. Plenty of taxes levied on business are passed on to the consumer in the form of higher prices: excises on freight and fuels, property and income taxes imposed on just about every profitable corporation. There is simply no way to gauge the effect on the average householder of these "hidden" imposts.*

So the American who thinks he is only in a 20 percent tax bracket is being conned. The boys in Washington do everything they can to hide the cost of government from those who pay the freight. The conn*ors* live in mortal fear that the con*ees* will figure out that government services are not the bargain they might think.

How much do you think you paid in taxes last year? Well, think again. The Tax Foundation reported in its most recent issue of *Facts and Figures on Government Finance* that "Government expenditures for 1977 are projected at $9,607 per U.S. household." This is the average of all taxes collected by all government (federal, state, and local) from you and me. If you don't remember writing out a check for that amount, or having it deducted from your weekly paycheck, welcome to the club. You're beginning to realize how you are being plucked!

The Tax Foundation also confirms that "the good old days" actually were pretty good, at least when it comes to how much money bureaucratic leeches drained from working Americans. Back in 1940, total government expenditures per family came to a lowly $308 per year. By 1950 they had climbed to $1,650—still a pretty affordable sum. By 1960 they were approaching $5,000 per year; in 1970 they passed the almost incredible total of $7,500 per family per year. And by the time you read this, government will spend over $10,000 per family per year. And one way or another, every cent of that amount comes from your pocket.

That's a lot of hamburgers and Cokes, or pizzas and beer. In fact, it's a lot of *anything!* It's the new car you couldn't afford to buy. The down payment on a home you couldn't afford to make. It's braces for your nine-year old—or two years of college for your high-school graduate. It's money you won't be able to save for your retirement. You won't be able to spend it at all, because government has already done it for you.

It's almost enough to make a snowman's blood boil, isn't it? When you realize that the median family income for 1978 is expected to be just over fourteen thousand dollars, that government outlay of ten thousand dollars per household takes on terrifying proportions.

Using the Hillendahl figures, which allow for indirect taxation, the average worker toils from January first to June sixth for Big Brother. The historically minded will recall that June sixth was D-Day, when the Allied forces invaded Normandy. That should help you remember that June sixth is now T-Day—tax freedom day. You work from January first until June sixth to keep the country's spendaholics in green booze.

Representative Philip Crane (R.-Ill.) observed recently that back in the Middle Ages a serf, whom we regard as the next thing to a slave, was required to turn over about thirty percent of the fruit of his labor to the lord of the manor. Now that Americans are taxed almost fifty percent of our incomes, Congressman Crane says we'd have to *reduce* government spending to reach a position equal to that of a medieval serf!

Whether you know it or not, taxes are the biggest item in your family budget. In 1977, on a per capita basis, the American family paid more in taxes that it did for food, shelter and clothing combined. And taxes are *rising* faster than any part of our budget!

In 1976, the Consumer Price Index showed the following increases in prices: food, up 3.1 percent; clothing, an added 3.3 percent; housing jumped 5.5 percent; new cars were up 6.3 percent; and gasoline and motor oil rose 4.1. During that same year, taxes soared an incredible 17.6 percent! Is it any wonder that more than four million Californians voted for Proposition 13?

And taxpayers from every other state, who know their backs are against the wall, asked how they could do the same thing? As Stanley Modic commented in *Industry Week:* "If boycotts are in order, perhaps we should begin with the prime cause of our inflation, taxes."

America is rapidly being turned into a taxocracy in which a person toils directly or indirectly almost six months a year for government. As Professor Wisdumb says in the comic strips: "In just fifty years we've gone from a chicken in every pot to a hand in every pocket." And the percentage of the chicken pie consumed by the gluttons on the Potomac continues to rise.

This year the Washington machine will be gobbling our dreams of personal success and achievement at the rate of $1.5 billion a day, spending at the rate of more than 12 thousand dollars per second. This year's jump of $50 billion in federal spending is going to add $750 in direct and hidden taxes on your family. If the government gets any more generous with its "free goodies" from Washington, we'll all be broke.

From the politician's point of view, the name of the game is to convince the voters that they are receiving more money from the government than they are paying in taxes. Human nature being what it is, people are happy if they think they are getting something that somebody else must pay for. It's when voters realize they are giving someone else the fruits of their own labor that they turn nasty. Too often, your "free lunch" paid for by someone else is good; the "free lunch" for your neighbor paid for by you is bad. In reality, there is no such thing as a "free lunch." And until the majority of voters face up to this somewhat unpleasant fact of life, it will be impossible to control the runaway growth of government.

Let us do something which politicians hate. Let's get

down to basics. Let's discuss some principles—principles which can be ignored, but not repealed. Most of us would not sneak into our neighbor's bedroom in the middle of the night and rifle his wallet. That is stealing. Everybody recognizes that it is stealing. It is immoral and illegal. Not even the most wild-eyed of our "Liberal" spenders advocates outright burglary.

But what is patently wrong on a one-on-one basis suddenly becomes praiseworthy when a politician promises to get the tax collector to do the stealing. Now, all of a sudden, this is not theft, it is *democracy*. Let the politicians and the tax collectors do the burglarizing and suddenly it's commendable!

The truth is that any economic gain *you* receive which someone else is forced to pay for is theft. It is a violation of the Biblical commandments against theft and against coveting.

Where does the process of using politicians to steal ultimately lead? Well, obviously no one is going to take the plundering of the fruits of his labors lying down. He will organize his friends to get a set of politicians to rip-off someone else in return. Soon, everybody is trying to "get their share"—that is, getting something from someone else, through the use of politicians. Naturally, the politicians love this process. They are only too happy to win votes through subsidies—to farms and factories, kiddies and grandpops, railroads and real estate developments, highways and hospitals, the list is virtually endless.

Everybody wants to steal more than is being stolen from him. But, for almost all of us, this is impossible. To understand why, let us imagine that there are 100 of us lined up in a circle. We are all picking the pocket of the person in front of us and whoever is behind us in line is picking our pocket. Everybody is trying to steal more than is being stolen from him.

But in a crowd like this, there will inevitably be some big bullies who will overwhelm the weaker ones. So some of the people must go to the middle of the circle to supervise the thievery. These theft organizers (let's call them government bureaucrats) have to be supported, too. So it is virtually impossible to come out ahead in the ring-around-the-rosey stealing game.

In real life, one out of five wage earners in America works for government. Naturally, he must be supported by the other four. Then there are the big-time manipulators who get the multi-million dollar government contracts and subsidies. They know how to skim off the cream—and a lot of the milk. It doesn't leave much for you and me! In fact, it is impossible for anyone in the middle class to come out ahead in the taxation vs. government benefits ball game. You've got a better chance buying a used car from a guy named Tricky Dick.

Why do the voters allow it to continue? Politicians, if nothing else, are sly. They do everything possible to camouflage the impact of their spending. They are past masters at devising a myriad of schemes to hide from the taxpayer the real cost of government.

Besides trying to pull the wool over the eyes of the taxpaying sheep they are shearing, the politicians stand ready with a number of phony solutions to propose whenever the bleating becomes too loud. The idea is to cater to the general feeling of every taxpayer that he pays too much in taxes while others do not pay enough. Senator Russell Long, Chairman of the powerful Senate Finance Committee, has remarked that most of the time tax reform means: "Don't tax you, don't tax me. Tax the fellow behind that tree." The name of the game is pin the tax tail on some other donkey.

This is one of the great games politicians play. Let people think the rich will pay for what you get. Everybody says, "What the heck, the rich can afford it. It is all right to steal from them. After all, the rich steal from the middle class, don't they?" How can you steal from me? I have nothing left to steal. The truth is that both the rich and the middle class are tax slaves.

The cry of "soak the rich" has incredible demagogic appeal. Reality, however, is something else. Internal Revenue Service figures for 1975 show that the top half of the taxpaying public paid nearly 93 percent of the income tax bill for the country.

But who are the "rich" who are to be soaked? The top ten percent of the taxpayers in income? If so, for 1975 you are talking about taxpayers with an income of $23,420 or more. This tenth of the taxpaying public paid almost half of the total tax bill for 1975. Five years earlier, the top tenth had paid 45 percent of the taxes.

Or perhaps you'd prefer to broaden the definition a little and take in the top quarter. The fourth of the population with the highest incomes—$15,898 and up in 1975—paid nearly three-quarters of the federal income tax load. That was up, by the way, from slightly more than two-thirds of the tax load just five years earlier.

Do we continue to shift the load of paying for government until the upper quarter is paying four-fifths of the bills? Nine-tenths? The works?

Naturally, the populist orators do not want their listeners to think in terms of soaking the "rich" $15,898-a-year man. The millionaire is supposed to be the one who gets it, the sly got-rocks who is presently slipping unscathed through the IRS net.

Well, even that fairy tale doesn't hold up when IRS statistics are examined.

It turns out that the number of income million-aires—those earning a million or more in 1975—was only 1,149. While people up in that earning bracket have access to better tax men and tax shelters than the rest of us, they obviously left a lot of their money behind in the net as they went through.

The average taxpayer in this top thousand-plus paid out $1,011,317 in income taxes in 1975. That's a heavy levy per person. But there are so few of such persons that altogether their taxes totaled just over a billion dollars. At current rates of spending, their taxes will run the federal government about *one day!* Even con-fiscating their entire income would pay the federal bills for less than a week. The other 360 days somebody else foots the bill. And mostly that somebody else is you and me.

Next to "soaking the rich," another most popular fable which the politicians use to try to confuse the tax suckers is the idea that the corporations will pick up the tab for the handouts most people want. As we've already pointed out, all the taxes which corporations pay are passed on to the consumer. They have to be. Otherwise, the company would go out of business.

It is ironic that with taxation gobbling up almost fifty cents on each dollar spent, the "Liberal" Establishment and its army of media flacks keep chanting about the "huge profits" being made by business. Yet profits, which are vital to industrial growth and job creation, are about ten percent of the sum which goes to taxes.

The effects of government taxation as it ripples through the economy are very complicated. Irwin Schiff sums up the situation in his book, *The Biggest Con,* in this fashion:

America is being poisoned by a tax system that (1)

penalizes economic efficiency and destroys incentive while subsidizing inefficiency and encouraging unemployment, (2) diverts the nation's supply of capital to less efficient areas, (3) destroys jobs, (4) increases substantially the difficulty of the older workers to find employment, (5) promotes greater concentrations of economic power, (6) compels those entering business to make Uncle Sam a "silent partner" who puts up no capital yet demands more than half the profits, and (7) contributes directly to a lowering of public morality while increasing the influence of organized crime....

We are fast approaching the point where the problem will become irreversible. As a widely circulated study by the Ford Motor Company shows, there are already more people dependent on government for a livelihood than there are productive workers in private industry paying taxes.

Where will it end? In 1974, Roy Ash, then Federal Budget Director, estimated that by the year 2000, combined federal-state-local budget outlays would account for 80 percent of personal income. How hard would *you* work if government took 80 percent of everything you earned? What about your neighbor? Think he'll keep his nose to the grindstone then? But if you won't work and he won't—who will?

The war of the unproductive against the productive has no limit. The vast majority of the 16.8 million people who are employed by the government will fight like wildcats to preserve their jobs. Most of the 61.3 million other people drawing government checks will vociferously resist any move which they feel might jeopardize their welfare check, subsidy or whatever. Most of the millions of teenagers who have been given the vote have little to lose, and thus will opt for supporting more government spending programs.

All we have to do is look at England to see where this insanity will wind up. Great Britain, once energetic and productive, isn't so great anymore. It has been reduced to a general state of ugliness, envy, and whining, with its most capable and productive citizens fleeing in droves. The island country would have gone belly up years ago had it not been for life-saving infusions of loans from the United States. If you check the taxation tables, you will see that America is trailing behind England by about ten to fifteen years. For example, England hit the 45 percent tax take of total income in 1965. This is the position we are in today.

Another factor which is not encouraging is a poll taken in England which showed 82 percent favored reductions in taxes. Yet the same people turn around and vote for politicians who promise more "benefits" and thus inevitably higher taxes. "There is no such thing as a free lunch." That truism should be carved on every school and public building in America. But even in unmerry old England, people still like to think that the ham sandwich won't be paid for by charging more for the ale.

This is where we are headed, unless a change is made—and fast. The standard of living will continue to decline. There will be stagnation in the economy. And politicians will promise to "get things moving again." Their formula will be to hike federal spending—which will just make things worse.

We demand more from government and government demands more from business but, says Walter Hansen, chairman of Pete, Marwick, Mitchell & Co., we fail to see that, "The closer the effective tax rate approaches 100 percent, the closer it is that tax revenues, production, and job creation approach zero."

We are being enslaved with our own money. If the spending orgy isn't stopped, if we do nothing, we shall inevitably have nothing.

Are we doomed to be tax slaves? Is there no way out? If the situation is to get better, we Americans are going to have to stop kidding ourselves. We will have to face the real world—not the one of pleasant delusions that is so often projected by politicians.

The first reality is that there is no such thing as a free lunch. The second is that we must think in terms of *cutting* taxes and spending, not just shifting the burden to someone else. Government expenditures always rise to meet whatever income is available. Or more! The government's voracious appetite for money can never be satisfied. The only way to cut government waste and extravagance is to *cut government income*. It's been done in California, and now it's time to do it on the federal level.

Supertaxing, superspending, supergovernment will only be stopped when members of the House of Representatives (where all spending bills begin) vote to stop it. This is the only tax reform that will work. The Congressmen who are busy buying votes with your money are not going to solve the problem. They need to be retired to other pastures. But few will go voluntarily—they know the grass isn't greener elsewhere. Most of them have never had a job as financially and egotistically rewarding as being a Congressman. That means you are going to have to go to work in *your* Congressional district, campaigning for effective tax reform.

Chapter Three
Debt, Here Is Thy Sting

As we said at the beginning of Chapter Two, there are only three ways the Money Moochers in Washington can cover their spending sprees. They must either take the money away from the people in the form of taxes, borrow the amount necessary to make up the shortfall, or they can cause more money to be printed. Let's look briefly at method two: the government's borrowing policies.

The redistribution by Congress of other people's earnings makes the recipients happy. But paying high taxes makes people unhappy. They will tolerate heavy taxes only so long as they cling to the fiction that they are getting more from the government than they are putting in. The politicians do not dare raise taxes further (except in the case of Social Security, which we shall discuss in a later chapter). The last thing they want to do is pour more fuel on taxpayer rebellion fires that are already burning.

To perpetuate the fiction that people get more from the government than they pay for, the politicians regularly spend billions more than they collect in taxes. The difference between what the government spends and what it collects during a fiscal year is the deficit. The National Debt is the total of all deficits piled up over the years.

Because the debt and its effects are hidden from the average taxpayer, running a deficit helps the politicians with their hoax that people are receiving more from the government than they pay in taxes. In the long run, however, this is the most expensive kind of federal spending, as we shall see.

Our politicians have turned the United States into a giant debtocracy. Under the Washington spendathon, debt is rising faster than corn in Kansas. Consider: In eight years Harry Truman increased the national debt $4.5 billion; two terms of Dwight Eisenhower added $16 billion of red ink; eight years of the Kennedy-Johnson Administrations piled on $55 billion; the Nixon-Ford years quadrupled that total. And now, in just two years, President Jimmy Carter has added nearly $100 billion to the National Debt.

Do you detect a trend here?

Richard Nixon originally campaigned as Mr. Frugal. As a candidate he proclaimed:

> *For five years this (Johnson) Administration has refused to keep federal spending within federal means.*
>
> *The total deficit run up in the budgets of the Johnson-Humphrey years will amount to more than $55 billion. This massive deficit has wracked and dislocated the economy....*
>
> *There is nothing the matter with the engine of free enterprise that cannot be corrected by placing a prudent and sober engineer at the throttle.*

As it turned out, a $55 billion deficit made LBJ look like the Penny Pincher of the Pedernales. Not that the talk did not continue for a while. When introducing his first budget, the Sultan of San Clemente promised "to balance the federal budget so you can balance the family budget." These noble words were not, unfortunately, backed with equally noble deeds.

Eight Nixon-Ford budgets added an incredible $247 billion to the national debt! It took the government from 1787 to 1945—158 years and two World Wars—to increase the debt as much as Presidents Nixon and Ford did in only eight. Incredibly, these red ink fiascos were run up by the party which always runs for office claiming fiscal integrity. That is akin to honoring Wiley Coyote for his efforts on behalf of endangered Road Runners!

The supposedly prudent pachyderms always wail that they *couldn't help it.* Congress was run by Liberal Democrats. True. But both Nixon and Ford came under great fire from conservative Congressmen in their own party for introducing budgets with huge, *planned* deficits. Ford used the veto occasionally to keep the spending-deficit situation from going completely berserk, but on the whole there was little leadership from the White House to control federal spending and thereby limit the exploding federal debt.

Of course, nobody more sophisticated than Baby Snooks expects leaner budgets from the Democrats. It is true that Jimmy Carter *campaigned* on the promise to balance the federal budget. But that promise went out the window a lot faster than Peter Bourne—and the smell was not nearly as sweet as the good Doctor's funny cigarettes.

The debt Mr. Carter will place on us this year is more red ink than was accumulated from the founding of the country through the middle of World War II. While the Peanut Politico *promised* to balance the federal budget, this year he will miss the mark by $1 billion *per week.*

Jimmy's first two trips to bat in the budget derby led to homeruns for the enemy, as he racked up over $100 billion in deficits. His chances of reducing these $50-billion-a-year deficits to zero in the next two years are about as good as Brother Billy's quest for the presidency of the Women's Christian Temperence Union.

These monstrous deficits have been piled up despite the fact that we are now employing in the marketplace the highest percentage of our population (forty-one percent) in American history—and both individual and corporate taxes are at an all-time high. But even with more taxpayers paying more taxes than ever before, government expenditures exceed tax revenue by over $50 billion dollars.

By the end of 1978, *U.S. News & World Report* estimates, the federal debt will be $785 billion—over three-quarters of a trillion dollars. More than half of this will have been accumulated since 1970. Project this out over another decade and where do you think we will be? And, *USN&WR* says that by 1982 the debt will hit *one trillion dollars*. The interest *alone* on that much debt will be $75 billion or more! Surely this madness cannot continue for long.

One of the incredible things about all this is that the public is so numbed that very few believe anything can be done about all this fiscal insanity. There was more furor over a $4 billion Eisenhower deficit than there is about the Man with the Pepsodent Smile shoving us up to the trillion-dollar mark. This is apparently because the vast majority of our citizens, including the majority of Congressmen, have no idea of what this means and what the consequences will be. People say to themselves, "Well, we're still here so I guess the deficits are not as harmful as some people have claimed."

The consequences are real, predictable, and very, very certain. We'll discuss some of them shortly. But first, some more bad news. For the deficits are actually worse than these figures reveal.

In 1974, the nation's largest accounting firm, Arthur

Anderson & Co., did a study of the federal government's accounting methods. After completing the study, they urged the government to do just like corporations do—use an accrual system which more accurately matches assets with liabilities. According to Anderson & Co., if the money manipulators in Washington used standard accounting procedures—required *by law* for all large corporations—and included real federal liabilities in calculating the federal shortfall, a much different picture would emerge. Many items are "off budget" and do not show on the books. But these obligations are just as real as the money you owe Master Charge.

The year 1974 was Nixon's best. He only ran a deficit of $3.5 billion. At least that is all that showed on the books. According to honest and realistic accounting methods, Anderson & Co. said the *true* deficit for that year was a blockbuster $95 billion. Moreover, Anderson & Co. figured that the government's total assets in 1974 were $329 billion. Not a paltry amount, I'm sure you'll agree. But federal *liabilities* were over $1.1 trillion! That's a difference of $811 billion! It's enough to make an embezzler look like a church deacon by comparison.

A second study, done for fiscal 1976, revealed another bad year for the government. Under the accrual method of accounting, the government had an operating deficit of $85.2 billion. Using its customary cash accounting method, the government reported a deficit of *only* $65.6 billion.

This kind of honest accounting would highlight for our legislators, particularly the free spenders, the unfunded liabilities they have obligated you and me to pay. A bill proposing Truth in Government Accounting was submitted by Congressman Philip M. Crane. The

Crane Bill was about as popular with his colleagues as a Salvation Army Band at a Hugh Hefner party. Will it surprise you to learn that Arthur Anderson has *not* been asked to do any more studies of federal accounting procedures? Yes, the whiz kids in Washington know exactly what they are doing. In fact, during a recent Senate debate on federal budgetary practices, Sen. Warren Magnuson turned to his colleagues and said, "I suppose the SEC would put us in jail if we were a corporation."

Bad economics can mean good politics—that is, reelection at the polls—when the public does not understand what is happening. The politician's motto is: "Get the vote today—who cares about tomorrow?" A Congressman can vote for benefits which will not be paid for decades hence. He takes the bows as a noble humanitarian and collects the votes from grateful constituents. By the time the bill comes due, the *public servant* will be long gone. It is sort of a "Fly now and pay later" proposition, as we shall see when we discuss Social Security.

One of the great hypocrisies of all time is the so-called "Legal Debt Limit." Every time the red ink budget pushes up against the laughable "temporary ceiling," Congress goes through a lot of soul-searching, desk pounding, fervent debate, and pious promises. Then it always—but *always*—votes to raise the legal debt limit. If Congress ever refused to raise the debt ceiling, the federal paychecks would come to a grinding halt. You can imagine how likely the politicians are to let that happen.

The federal legal limit is a hoax, a fraud. It's a joke ... but you're not laughing about it, are you?

You may remember when our political benefactors were telling us that the National Debt was nothing to be concerned about. After all, they said, "We owe it to ourselves." You don't hear that one very often anymore, do you? This is because interest on the National Debt is now the third-largest item in the federal budget, exceeded only by social welfare and defense. In 1965 the payment due for money borrowed in the past was just over ten billion dollars. By 1976 the single-year tab had escalated to $44.6 billion—greater than the total annual *sales* of General Motors. By 1982, says *U.S. News & World Report,* the annual interest on money the politicians have wasted in past years will be an unbelievable $65 billion. A chart of the increasing cost to the taxpayer of the National Debt looks like a rocket taking off for Mars. Yet only the naive believe it will ever be paid. It will merrily compound until either the debt overwhelms us or our currency becomes worthless.

If you divide up the admitted national debt on a per capita basis, it means you owe yourself $3,511 for the government's debt. That works out to about $14,044 for the typical family of four. This is double the per capita debt of just a dozen years ago. Your share of the *true* national debt, of course, is much, much higher. Do you really think you just owe it to yourself? Then why do international bankers, Arabian oil sheiks, and the big investment houses on Wall Street keep collecting it? Anyone send you *your* share lately?

The old chestnut that "we owe it to ourselves" is a cruel hoax, of course. Foreigners hold many billions of that debt. Rather than keep the billions of dollars that have piled up in foreign central banks as a result of our adverse trade balances, our government has over the years convinced foreign governments to convert their dollars into U.S. bonds. Arab governments, for example, have purchased more than $17 billion in short-term federal notes in the past six months. Congressional spokesmen now say that more than one-fourth of federal short-term securities are held by foreign governments or foreign corporations. In the case of another Mideast war, foreign holders of U.S. securities might well exert catastrophic influence over our money market as a lever on foreign policy, creating a financial panic by dumping their notes. If they do, God help us!

Our friends in Washington would like us to believe that the national debt is sustained by millions of little people buying their Savings Bonds and, as the TV commercials say, "taking stock in America." Of course, when you buy stock in a private company, you are purchasing part ownership. When you buy a government bond, you are taking over part of the debt. Historically, when well-meaning, patriotic souls have held their bonds to maturity, they have actually *lost* real purchasing power.

Individuals own only about 12 percent of the debt. The bulk of the debt is owned by the federal government itself through Social Security and other government trust funds. But it is strictly a paper proposition. The government has spent the money and replaced it with an I.O.U. If *you* could operate the same way, you could live very high on the proverbial hog. But don't try it: The very same thing our government does manipulating money is a crime for anyone else!

There is another major consequence of the spendocrats swilling down a fifth of Old Deficit every day. As we said before, there are only two ways the government can obtain money to support its deficits. It either has to borrow the cash or print it. Both have terrible consequences for the economy and the taxpayers. If the government borrows money out of the economy to give away to welfreeloaders, then that money cannot be used as capital. Just as a farmer is more productive when he uses a tractor than when he tills the soil by hand, so workers are more productive when capital is invested in better plants and equipment. The surest way to higher wages is more production. In the modern world, productivity is chiefly increased by new equipment and improved technology. Thus, bleeding off capital by government holds down wages and prevents the creation of jobs.

If the money goes to social-welfare programs instead of capital goods, most of it evaporates in instant consumption. Senator William Proxmire, Chairman of the Senate Committee on Banking, Housing and Urban Affairs, has pointed out that for every $10 billion drained from capital supplies by federal borrowing, there will *not* be private capital for approximately five hundred thousand new housing starts. That causes a direct loss of one million jobs and an indirect loss of two million more. The more money the government has to borrow, the more jobs that are destroyed or never come into being. Money that is loaned to the U.S. Government cannot be loaned to the Amalgamated Widgets Corporation to create more and better widgets. And our own standard of living, instead of going up, starts to drop. You and I are caught between the taxation rock and the inflation hard place.

In the next thrilling chapter, we will discuss the government's deficits as a cause of inflation. But while we are dealing with debt, we should mention that inflation is a major cause of *personal* debt, as families struggle in vain to preserve their standard of living. Private debt a decade ago was $961.3 billion. Now it is $2.5 *trillion*. Federal, state, and local debt is another trillion dollars (using the government's dishonest $700 billion national debt figure). At the rate that private and public debt is escalating, it will hit an astounding $6 trillion in 1985.

The implications of this are frightening. As Richard Russell, author of the highly respected *Dow Theory Letter,* said in his December 1977 issue:

> *What worries me is that at this point the U.S. has simply* used up its capital. *Everything, and I mean everything, is awash in debt. The cities and municipalities, the citizens, the corporations, the banks, all of it is "loaned out."*

Debt, where is thy sting? If we don't force about 300 Congressmen and Senators to change the way they vote—or change *them* for someone who will vote to protect us—we will find out the hard way.

Chapter Four
The Great Inflation Robbery

Of all the problems facing the country, more people are more concerned about inflation than any other. Worry over the exploding cost of living surpasses even the fear of crime. Every time you go to buy something it seems the price has taken another jump. Families are discovering that there is more and more month left at the end of the paycheck.

The cause is very simple: When the government spends more money than it is willing to tax its citizens, it must either borrow or print the money which it uses to make up the deficits. Financing deficits is the very heart of the inflation problem.

Politicians put the blame for inflation on everyone but themselves. Republicans blame greedy labor unions; Democrats decry greedy businessmen. Actually, both are victims of the politicians and bureaucrats. The latter naturally want to shift the fault to someone else, lest the public unceremoniously retire them to growing petunias. Some politicians even have the nerve to blame consumers for inflation. The current scapegoat is Arab oil sheiks. Nobody likes them. This pin-the-tail on some other donkey ploy is one of the greatest con jobs in the history of bunco scams. And that takes some doing. P.T. Barnum never got away with the kind of hoax that politicians do with their inflation-fraud rhetoric.

The key to this shell game is that the vast majority of our citizens do not understand the real definition of inflation. In a recent CBS Special ("INFLATION: How Much, How Long?"), commentator John Hart began by defining inflation. He said defining inflation is the only easy aspect of the problem. "Inflation," quoth Hart, "is a period of rising prices." To the man on the street, who has relied on the media for what he knows of economics, that definition might seem self-evident. Unfortunately, it is wrong. Who says so? Every honest economist says so, and so does your dictionary. *Webster's New World Dictionary,* for example, defines inflation as "an increase in the amount of currency in circulation, resulting in a relatively sharp and sudden fall in its value and rise in prices: it may be caused by an increase in the volume of paper money issued or of gold mined."

Read that carefully. Inflation is an increase in the supply of paper money which causes prices to rise.

If only CBS had the Hart to tell us the real truth. The mass media helps the politicians to cover their crime by using the term "inflation" as a *synonym* for the rising cost of living. Walter Cronkite will tell you that *inflation* was two percent last month because food, clothing, and steel went up in price. The public responds as planned by getting angry at those who produce food, clothing and steel. This is a fraud and a hoax. Though related, the cost of living index and inflation are two different things. Who increases the money supply? Butchers, bakers, and candlestick makers? Certainly not. The supply of money is controlled by the federal government and its Federal Reserve System. It is *carefully* controlled. So that we never have inflation unless the government *wants* to have inflation and acts to create it. As economist John Kamin observes:

Government started inflation through deficit

financing and removal of all currency backing. Not
one in one thousand knows what's happening. The
talk about interest, labor, capital spending, housing
starts, etc., is smoke screen, the trappings of infla-
tion. The heart of the matter is deterioration of the
currency unit.

When more and more paper dollars are created out of
thin air by Washington, the *value* of all money drops.
As dollars drop in value, the Japanese want more of
them for their television sets; Germans want more of
them for automobiles; Arabs want more for oil. Domestic producers insist on receiving more dollars for their
goods. Workers demand more pay. We see the
symptoms—higher prices for products, services, and
wages—and are told we've seen the cause!

Higher prices are a *result* of inflation, not the cause.
Blaming the wage-price spiral for causing inflation is
probably the biggest of the Big Lies that politicians and
bureaucrats have used to camouflage their own actions. If the blame for inflation can be placed on unions,
or business, or the Arabs, or anyone *except* the policy-
makers in Washington, then those who created the
problems in the first place will be safe. In fact, they will
probably be shouting the loudest and longest that we
should now trust them to come up with the solutions!

If only the Carters and Cronkites would tell the
truth. But their hoax serves their commitment to ever
bigger government. The government inflates the
money supply to meet its deficits, and that bids up
prices and causes the cost of living to rise. Food, clothing, and steel go up because the value of the currency
goes down. The producers are not to blame, as the
Cronkites and Carterites would have us believe. They
are among the *victims* of the government's legalized

counterfeiting. Business can't print new money. Nor can unions. Or the Arabs. Nor can *anyone* except the government in Washington.

The government has created these enormous amounts of new money, all unbacked by gold or silver, in two ways. The first is through expansion of bank credit by way of the Federal Reserve System. The second is through the enormous budgetary deficits, which are largely backed by bonds sold to the Federal Reserve System itself or to commercial banks. In both cases, these bonds are "monetized" (*i.e.*, turned into new money) and pumped into the economy.

Congressman Bud Schuster (R.-Pa.) explains how the National Debt causes inflation:

> *When the Government spends more than it takes in, it has to find the difference somewhere to pay the bills. The Treasury does the only thing it can do, since the President and Congress made financial commitments in excess of their means. Treasury tries to borrow the money.*
>
> *When the deficit is so big that the Treasury can't sell enough government bonds or notes to the American people without causing interest rates to rise too high, the Treasury raises the money it needs to pay the Government's bills in a very unique way. The Treasury Department sells its bonds or notes to the Federal Reserve System, which is the…agency that controls the supply of money in America. And get this—the Federal Reserve literally prints up more money on the government printing presses and pays it to the Treasury in exchange for the bonds which the Treasury printed up. The Treasury then takes this new money and pays the Government's debts …*

What we have is a money system under which the greater the government's debt, the more money the government releases to spend! How would you like to operate your household on such a basis? Wouldn't it be great to go down to Sears & Sawbuck, charge everything that catches your fancy, and then return home and print up the money to pay the bills? You can try this, of course. But if you're caught, the outfit that *legally* counterfeits the money will put you away in the crowbar motel.

You thought you were carrying money around in your pocket? Actually, it is the unsecured and unredeemable debt of the government. We have switched from money to debt as a medium of exchange! And the politicians keep printing more and more of this debt-money, as they seek to buy the votes for their own reelections. Look at the money in your wallet. On the bills it says Federal Reserve Note. A note is an instrument of debt. If we paid off the National Debt, technically we would have no circulating currency, because all Federal Reserve notes would have to be withdrawn!

Writing in *Dividing The Wealth* about the effects of this increase in currency, economist Howard Kershner observes: "When government adds to the supply of money, causing prices to rise, it is in reality confiscating a part of the wealth of its thrifty citizens. Those who have bank accounts, mortgages, bonds, life insurance, annuities or pensions lose a part of the *results* of their thrift."

That $120 billion dollars in new money which the Carter Administration has sluiced into the economy took on a value *only* by subtracting from the value of all the other money already in circulation. When the government prints dollars to cover its deficits, the introduction of that currency in the economy lowers the value of all the dollars already in circulation.

You can see why the politicians want to keep the public confused about inflation. You can see why the politicians look for scapegoats for the consequences of their flooding the economy with funny money. The $60 billion dollars which the 1979 Budget is likely to run in the red will gradually be turned into new green-ink money, which will also compete for goods and services.

As we have said, the "Liberal" media and the politicians have tried to cover for what is happening by creating a "guilt triangle" pitting business, labor, and private consumers against one another in a donnybrook over which is to blame for "inflation." It is all absurd, because *none* of those three groups has the ability to inflate the money supply. Only government can do it, and government is *increasing* rather than decreasing the deficit spending which really causes inflation.

Changes in supply and demand can also affect the price of a particular item, of course. But you cannot have *every* price leaping upward unless the government is increasing the money supply. This is not just economic theory. It is physics. You can't fill a quart jug with a pint of water. The media and the politicians wring their hands over the "wage-price" spiral on which they blame inflation. his is like saying that wet streets cause rain or that a falling thermometer causes a freeze.

Let us make the cause of the "wage-price spiral" perfectly clear. First, let us deal with wages. Let us suppose that you, prolific parent that you are, have ten children. On Saturday morning you line them up in your kitchen and assign each a chore. You have on a plate ten cookies, and to each you promise a cookie upon completion of his assigned task. The next week you

begin the same routine, but one of your more obstrep-
erous kidlets (the one that reminds you so much of your
mother-in-law) announces that she will not work unless she is paid two cookies. Upon which the rest of the
moppet brigade (all rather like your wife's side of the
family, really) demand that their cookie salaries be
doubled.

Alas, you are forced to inform them that you only
have ten cookies and therefore there is no way you can
raise their wages to twenty cookies unless your wife
increases the cookie supply by baking more cookies.
Without more baking, you can only give some of your
gang more cookies if you give others less cookies. You
cannot have a general rise in cookie wages in your
mini-economy unless you bake more cookies.

The same is true in the maxi-economy as the mini-
economy. You can't pay workers more money unless
there is more money available with which to pay them.

Now for prices. Imagine that you are at an auction.
As with the other people there, you have a certain
amount of money in your wallet with which to bid on
the things you want. Suddenly a man from government
bursts into the room carrying a bushel basket full of
newly printed money and proclaims the good news
that, without ever passing Go, you are all going to be
richer by two hundred dollars! Your rejoicing, however,
is short-lived. You thought you could buy more goods
with the additional greenbacks. But the money the
man from Uncle gave you did not increase the amount
of goods that are available to be auctioned. Supply and
demand have not changed, so you and the other people
at the auction now use your new money to bid against
each other for the goods that are for sale. The net result
is that the merchandise is bid up to heights that otherwise would not have been possible.

In the real economy, as at our auction, you cannot have a general rise in prices without an increase in the money supply. If new supplies of money are *not* printed, only an increase in production (a delivery at the auction of more goods) will result in your wages buying more of everything.

Does the above analogy of an auction apply to the real world? Yes! Our economy is simply a vast auction with millions of bids being made every day in a situation where prices are constantly fluctuating, not only because of normal changes in supply and demand, but because of ever-increasing distortions caused by the money printers in Washington.

You will recall that Mr. Webster informed us that inflation (an increase in the money supply) could be caused by either a rapid increase in the supply of paper money or gold. The world's supply of gold has increased only in miniscule amounts, but the supply of our paper money has been inflated (increased) by the proverbial leaps and bounds.

With the great increase in paper money, is it any surprise that the cost of living has been jumping like a nudist who sits on a hot stove? Remember the 5¢ Coke? Today it is 30¢. Remember going to the movies for a quarter? Recall the nickel bus ride which is now 50¢, or the dime magazine which now sells for a dollar? Gone are the days. Gone not with the wind, but with the printing press.

For years Administrations have been telling Americans that the worst of *inflation* (by which it means the rising cost of living) is nearly over. Everything will be just peachy the day after tomorrow. But mañana never comes. The Nixon gang used to proclaim that "inflation" would soon be down to an *acceptable* four percent. It never did. Now the Carterites are talking about slowing the rise in the cost of living to an "acceptable" six or seven percent.

During the past few years Federal Reserve Board Chairman Arthur Burns attempted to keep the growth of the money base at between 6 and 8 percent. This is now considered "conservative" and "cautious." Yet at an increase of 7.3 percent per year, the money supply will double in only a decade! But Arthur Burns is now out—removed, we are told, by Jimmy Carter because he would not expand (inflate) the money supply at a faster clip! Congressman James Collins points out:

> *With the Carter Administration and the liberal congressional congressional Democrats constantly increasing the size of the federal debt, there is no way we can avoid increased inflation. If this year's budget deficit is indicative of President Carter's future budgets, our national debt will double to $1.5 trillion in nine years. It is impossible for prices to remain stable or for business to expand when government is the biggest spender and the biggest business in the nation.*

Keep in mind that the government is going deeper in the red to the tune of over $1 billion every week. That billion will turn up as brand new money as the government spends it into the economy and it is re-spent by the recipients. Like at our imaginary auction, it will bid up the prices of goods and labor. There is a period called "lag time" before the new money pushes up your grocery bill. This *lag time* can be anywhere from six months to two years, so that a 8.75 percent increase in the money supply in 1978, for example, would not automatically mean an 8.75 percent increase in the cost of living during the same year. But, the damage is done and will eventually be paid for by you in everything you buy. It can only be offset by increases in national productivity. However, the same politicians who run up the deficits are also guilty of passing all kinds of laws creating giant bureaucracies which tie up the *productive* segments of our society in miles of red tape.

As Dr. Burns warned, the "mild" seven-percent inflation of 1977 has already given way to double-digit inflation. We have a very unstable situation which Dr. Gary North refers to as "the economics of addiction." Here is how it works:

In the 1930s a British Fabian Socialist named John Maynard Keynes sold President Franklin Roosevelt on the idea that he could get the economy out of the depression by deficit spending. The new money pumped into the economy would be spent and put idle capacity and unemployed people back to work. The theory was that in bad times the government would stimulate the economy with a shot of inflation, and in boom times it would tighten the supply of money and credit to cool things down. The theory was adopted lock, stock, and red ink by the academic community.

Needless to say, the politicians loved the theory, since it allowed them to play Santa Claus. In practice, however, the Keynesian perpetual-motion machine, which promised perpetual prosperity via the printing press, has been a disaster. It is the reason a nickel cup of coffee now costs a quarter. Now, we are at the point where we get the worst of all possible worlds, the inflationary boom followed by the inflationary recession. A new word has even been coined to describe our current dilemma — *stagflation*.

As Dr. North points out, the situation in our economy is analogous to that of the heroin addict. At first, a little shot makes him feel good. But, the fix soon wears off and he needs another injection of junk, just like the economy needs another injection of junk money. The stronger the addiction, the bigger the shot desired. Soon the addict demands bigger and more frequent injections, or he starts going through withdrawal symptoms.

The same thing holds true with the economy. Bigger deficits must be run up, to keep the economy from sinking into recession. For example, in 1954 President Eisenhower got the country out of a recession by running a $4 billion deficit. It took about $150 billion in deficits to get out of the 1974-75 recession.

It used to be years between recessions. Now, we hardly crawl out of one recession when we find ourselves sliding into another. By the early '80s, we can expect the government to have to run a half-trillion-dollar a year budget to get us out of a recession. That is a Big Fix, in more ways than one!

Clearly, the situation is out of control. Uncle Sam has a green monkey on his back and a lot of needle tracks on his arm. It should be obvious that if the Keynesian theory of spending ourselves into prosperity really worked, we would all own a Rolls Royce and a yacht by now. P.T. Barnum turned out to be right again. We've been played for suckers. The politicians' promise to give us something for nothing has turned out to be a perpetual debt machine which is now destroying the buying power of all our earnings and savings.

The dollar is dying. Today's ten cent mini-dollar will become the nickel micro-dollar a few years hence. Then it will become the one cent sub-micro-mini dollar. In a few years almost all of us may be millionaires. Somehow earning three-hundred thousand dollars a year loses a lot of its glamor, when you realize Big Macs will probably cost $25 each!

Arthur Burns, Chairman of the Federal Reserve Board until relieved by Jimmy Carter, told the House Banking Committee last year: "If we go the Latin American way, which is the way we seem to be going, then we will have interest rates on Latin American standards, that is, substantially higher."

What is the Latin American way? Leonard Greenwood described it for us in the *Los Angeles Times* in May 1974:

> *Brazil has suffered from inflation most of this century. Early in the 1960s it reached almost 100% a year and it was one of the factors that caused the military to take power in 1964. Since then tough monetary policies have brought inflation down each year, and fiscal devices such as annual salary increases and monetary correction on savings and investments have helped Brazilians to live with rising prices.*

This is how Greenwood described what happened to bring Brazil to its knees. As you read it, ask yourself if the same tune is now being played in the United States:

> *In the last months of President Emilio Garrastazu Medici's government, prices were artificially controlled for political purposes. Medici had promised to keep inflation down to 12%. As the year went on, it became obvious this was unrealistic, but in a vain attempt to meet the target the prices that producers, wholesalers and retailers were allowed to charge were rigidly controlled.*
>
> *The immediate result was a series of shortages as producers stockpiled to get better prices later, or the*

production of some items was stopped when they could not be made at the controlled price.

This caused food shortages that have still not been solved. Long lines formed at supermarkets to wait for meat, beans, onions and cooking oil.

Arthur Burns warned last year that "if past experience is any guide, the future of our country is in jeopardy. No country has been able to maintain widespread economic prosperity once inflation got out of hand." But recession is a greater liability to politicians than inflation, which they can blame on someone else. Therefore, there is an irresistible temptation to try to spend our way out of the economic downslide—that is, to fight declining production with more inflation.

Let's look at the consequences of this money mania on you and your family.

First of all, inflation is a tax—a particularly vicious tax which is especially hard on the old and the poor. As economist Milton Friedman notes, inflation is the one form of taxation that can be imposed without legislation. Politicians are among the principal beneficiaries of inflation because they can buy votes without raising taxes. You pay this sneaky tax every day at the grocery, hardware store, and the supermarket, not on April 15th. The inflation tax diverts the wrath of disgruntled taxpayers away from politicians. People get mad at the hardware store owner and the grocer.

Since the average American pays the equivalent of 44 percent of his income in direct and indirect taxes, when you add on the inflation tax of seven to ten percent, over half of our income goes to taxes!

Many people will point out that as the cost of living goes up, most people's pay goes up along with it. True. But, the dice are loaded in the inflation flim-flam. We have a graduated income tax. During the past few years, three-fourths of all typical wage hikes have been swallowed up by inflation. The rest has been taken by the tax men because a pay increase usually shoves the recipient into a higher tax bracket.

You are probably painfully aware that the standard of living for the average working American is going *down,* while his taxes are going up, up, up. We middle class Americans are the biggest victims. We are being hit with a combination of the progressive income tax and purposely created inflation. As Walter H. Campbell, consulting editor of *Industry Week,* explains in an article, "Fewer Poor Before Tax; More After":

> *Federal income, most state income, and estate taxes have "progressive" rate schedules. As the dollar amounts to be taxed increase, higher and higher rates of tax apply.*
>
> *Example: The worker with a $5,000 taxable income pays $810 in federal income taxes, or about 16 percent. When inflation doubles that taxable income, his tax moves up to $1,820, or more than 18 percent. When it doubles again, his tax jumps to $4,380, or about 22 percent.*
>
> *The barely comfortable are pushed up into tax brackets intended for the affluent. The affluent, if their incomes keep pace with inflation, are shoved into brackets intended for the very rich.*
>
> *The result: We have fewer poor before taxes; and more poor after taxes.*

Inflation takes a bigger bite in practically all of the taxes we pay. The housewife is acutely aware of the bigger sales tax she pays as prices rise. Real property is reassessed and requires a heavier tax. So does personal property. That rampaging tax increase does not show up in your cost-of-living index, because the Consumer Price Index blithely ignores direct taxes.

As Mr. Carter's deficit greenbacks hit the financial fan, we will gradually all be shoved ever closer to the top tax brackets — now 70 percent. The only winners in the inflation game are the politicians. This is why the War on Inflation from Washington will always be a "no-win" war, until the complexion of Congress is drastically changed.

This year the taxpayers will have to fork over an incredible $55 billion just in interest on the national debt. Fifty billion dollars is the equivalent of the *entire* budget when Harry Truman was in the White House!

The middle class is being squeezed out of existence by the taxation-inflation syndrome. Four million Americans are holding down two jobs to pay for the extravagances of our politicians. Nearly half of the wives in the country are forced to work in order to make ends meet. The typical family starting out today cannot afford to buy a home, while many older Americans, retired on fixed incomes, are being driven out of the homes they bought and paid for years ago!

Not all the effects of inflation are monetary. Henry Hazlitt, one of America's foremost economists, tells us that the massive deficits our politicians are creating quite literally breed crime:

> *During every great inflation there is a striking decline in both public and private morality.*
> *The chain of causation, from inflation to corruption to crime, is direct. In a free enterprise system, with an honest and stable money, there is dominantly a close link between effort and productivity, on the one hand, and economic reward on the other.*

Inflation severs this link. Reward comes to depend less and less on effort and production, and more and more on successful gambling and luck. For some, gambling finally comes to seem too chancy, and corruption or crime a surer path to quick reward.

Retired persons, widows, and others on fixed income may be decimated by inflation, but *they* suffer in relative silence. It is the unemployed in our inner cities who are being agitated in their displeasure to hurl Molotov cocktails. If it comes to a choice between these voting blocs, the aged or the urban minorities, which voting bloc do you think will win? (The elderly will probably be consoled, however, with promises of another increase in government benefits — which will only add more fuel to the fires of inflation.)

Millions upon millions of Americans are depending upon pension and retirement programs which are going to be worthless if something is not done soon. The magnitude of the problem is spelled out by the *Wall Street Journal* of November 11, 1977:

Ten of the top 100 corporations on the Fortune 500 have unfunded liabilities equal to a third or more of their net worth, and total uncovered benefits for all corporations exceed $50 billion. What has not yet dawned on corporate America is that its unfunded pension liabilities are only a part of this problem, and a relatively small part at that. Fifty billion dollars is peanuts compared with the other unfunded pension-fund liabilities that corporate America must also meet out of future earnings.

There is now $4.1 trillion in unfunded Social Security liabilities, almost $1 trillion in unfunded *federal government pensions, and a few hundred billion in unfunded state and local pension funds. Where is it to come from if not from business earnings?*

Federal, state and local governments are going to pay off all these promises, and they are going to do it by taxing away the output of productive enterprise. Nor is this something that is going to happen in the next century. Observe the Congress piling on Social Security tax rates. The future is now!

Then, the *Journal* goes on to say that, as bad as things look now, they could get a lot, lot worse:

As far as we know, there are only two possible solutions. One, which obviously is our second choice, is a Russian-type revolution somewhere down the line. The new American Bolsheviks would of course repudiate all these liabilities incurred by their predecessors. Our first choice would be to have the DJIA rise to about 2000. That is, the value of the assets in the pension-fund portfolio climbs so high that everyone is in the black.

The solution seems simple enough: Stop adding to the burdens of the capital stock, through taxation and regulation that invite it to produce less; then, begin stripping away the burdens previously imposed, thereby encouraging it to produce more.

Notice that even the staid old *Wall Street Journal* says that a revolution may sweep America if the economy is not freed from the hands of the politicians! We can win this revolution now, through the ballot box. If we don't use ballots now, as the *Journal* warns, someone else will be using bullets later.

The government has decimated the savings and investments of thrifty Americans. If the Dow Jones Averages is adjusted for inflation, there have been no real profits in the stock market since 1955. The Dow would have to triple before it would put investors in the black as far as purchasing power is concerned. And then they would still have to pay 50-percent capital gains tax. Get the feeling the game is rigged against you?

People who have entrusted their savings to banks, savings and loans, insurance policies or bonds have, almost literally, been raped. Let's assume that you are earning 6 percent on your savings. You will have to pay income tax on that interest, reducing your real net to 4 or 5 percent. But, the increase in the cost of living is at least double that! The value of your savings is systematically being wiped out.

So many thrifty, responsible people were being pushed to the walls—and sometimes through the walls and into the streets, as their homes had to be sold to pay skyrocketing property taxes—that the tax revolt was launched in California. More than four million Americans took the law into their own hands—legally and constitutionally — and said to the spendocrats, "No more. You *must* cut taxes ... now!" The same thing can be done to Washington. The Money Monster our politicians have created can be chained down—as our Founding Fathers meant it to be. The purpose of this book is to show you why—and *how*.

Chapter Five
The Welfare Wonderland

She used at least 15 aliases (one account says 80) and her trail of addresses snaked through fourteen states as she made a career of collecting welfare payments and food stamps. Over five years she pocketed at least $300,000. One estimate put her total take from all operations at almost $1 million. Once she applied for aid as the mother of seven pre-school children (two sets of twins and one of triplets). Her application was approved without question. When she finally came to the attention of authorities, she owned three automobiles and four buildings in Southside Chicago.

Meet Linda Taylor, "the welfare queen," whose high-living ways while exploiting every loophole in the "welfare mess" brought the need for "welfare reform" to public view again.

But cleaning up "the welfare mess," an ever-recurring political promise, is one of those faithfully parroted choruses of our times. It seems heavy in intent but is invariably slim in results. It's not that nothing can be done; the problem is that too many bureaucrats are afraid they may be swept out if any house cleaning does occur! They hold onto their empires harder than a bulldog gripping the postman's pants.

A Texas woman bilked the Medicaid program out of $100,000 by creating a fake clinic. One man in Michigan was charged with taking the Michigan Department of Social Services for a cool million dollars. In California, a band of ex-social workers was discovered running a school instructing others in the fine art of welfare cheating! Their take was 20 to 50 percent of their students' illicit gains.

In Alameda County, California, eight well-to-do women tested the dole system by posing as welfare mothers; all eight received aid and then tried to expose the unusually lax policies in the county.

In 1978, Medicare spokesmen informed the nation's taxpayers that their funds are being used, among other things, to pay $5,600 for a sex change operation for a San Diego man who had lived and dressed as a woman for the past three years. Thomas M. Tierney, Director of Health, Education and Welfare's Medicare Bureau, said a new policy extends Medicare coverage to "gender reassignment surgery," officially for "sex change," as long as the candidates "have at least one year's experience living as a member of the opposite sex."

Grand Jury and Supreme Court reports from New York City indicate that over a two-year period a billion dollars was wasted in Medicaid money in the Big Apple. Only one out of every 200 applicants was ever checked, nursing homes billed the city to care for dead patients, pharmacists short-changed impoverished clients, and dentists extracted thousands of teeth unnecessarily. More than a thousand dead New Yorkers were receiving welfare checks each month. As a tribute to the toughness of even the dearly departed in New York, it should be noted that every check was cashed, too!

If you shivered through the winter of 1977-78, with West Virginia coal miners striking the companies that could have helped alleviate the situation, you'll want to know that your tax monies provided $4.4 million per month in food stamps for the strikers. The combined outlay in welfare costs to help the strikers was $547 per striker, per month. With this kind of support, a strike can last a long time.

Across the nation, an increasingly work-shy younger generation has learned how to live off combined federal and state welfare, unemployment benefits, and "relief" for a year or more at a crack, by exploiting a system whose proponents now admit it is unmanageable.

Caspar W. Weinberger, chief of the bloated Department of Health, Education and Welfare during the Nixon era, came out of the experience a little shell-shocked. He learned that, even with the best intentions of cleaning it up, the "welfare mess" has become a monster of grotesque dimensions. It is, indeed, Dr. Frankenstein's creation run wild, a behemoth whose every movement saps more strength from our increasingly tax-bled nation. Said Weinberger on leaving Washington:

> *After five and a half years in various posts in Washington, I come away with a deep concern that if the enormous growth of our pervasive Federal government continues, it may take from us our personal freedom at the same time it shatters the foundations of our economic system.*
>
> *...More than half the budget is spent for Federal domestic social programs. These programs, consisting mainly of uncoordinated, spasmodic responses to a variety of needs, real and fancied, are threatening to bring us into national insolvency. They are also an increasing intrusion into the lives and affairs of all of us. The whole human resource field is under the lash of Federal law: doctors, hospitals, teachers, college presidents, students, volunteer agencies, city halls and state capitols—all are subject to this or that control from Washington.*

When the Founding Fathers put the phrase, "to promote the general welfare," in the Constitution, they were talking about the common good, such as defense, a post office, court systems, *etc.* They weren't talking about providing perpetual welfare by robbing hardworking Peters to provide for unproductive Pauls.

With social spending programs now accounting for 58% of the federal budget, the dimensions of the largesse have taken on mind-boggling proportions. The sum total of federal, state, and local bureaucrats involved in administering an annual outpouring of more than $440 billion in "relief" and social spending of all kinds now numbers 331,000. They shuffle through the paperwork that sends 23,400,000 citizens some kind of benefits regularly.

On May 1, 1978, a report disclosed that the federal part of this action is $248 billion per year to administer 182 "benefit programs"—or, phrased a different way, 69 cents of every tax dollar collected by the federal government as tax receipts in the last fiscal year went to indirect or direct "benefits"—such as those which dispensed so much easy money to Ms. Taylor. Some $60 billion per year goes to direct cash-assistance programs.

In twelve years, the Aid to Families with Dependent Children program has grown from $1.7 billion to $9.9 billion; Medicaid has swollen from $3.3 billion to $15 billion; and the Food Stamp rip-off has skyrocketed from a "modest" $35 million to $5.3 billion today, or a 16,000 percent jump!

The AFDC figures are doubly interesting because, while its grants quintupled between 1961 and 1969, the total child population increased by only a third. The AFDC growth can largely be traced to "absentee fathers" (estimated 590,000 in 1961 vs. 1,482,000 in

1973). Six out of seven paid no support whatsoever for their children. Many of them abandoned their families because the AFDC program actually made it *lucrative* to do so. Love 'em and leave 'em...to the taxpayers, that is.

A study by the Joint Economic Committee recently pointed out that, if an unemployed father deserted his family, the average gain, expressed in cash and food benefits, varied from $1,004 for a one-child family to $1,318 for a three-toddler unit. That is, the family had a *raise* in buying power if the father fled ... or appeared to. If there is any question why there are so many claims for AFDC payments, and a spiraling number of absentee fathers, one need look no further than the irresponsible actions of our Big Brother spendthrifts.

With billions being spread around like confetti at a wedding, the possibilities and potentials for cheating increase at a rate almost as fast as the amount of funds available to be spent.

There was, for example, $655 million worth of absolutely unnecessary surgery performed in fiscal year 1977 by physicians in the Medicaid scam. The program's projected net losses for 1977, through funds mishandling, was set at $2.6 billion; Medicare was not far behind with a $2.2 billion projected loss.

The much-maligned AFDC program in 1977 was but a piker alongside the phony claims and exorbitant fees charged by the Medicaid-Medicare rip-off specialists; a mere $699 million was lost through poor AFDC management. The Income Security and Supplemental Security Income programs came up with a projected combined loss through mishandling of $1.2 billion.

In fact, the investigators admitted, the projected yearly net loss from the well-intentioned effort to create more jobs, and to rescue Americans from some definition of "poverty," now comes to $15 billion a year. This is more than the gross national products of most states and many foreign countries! These are not *my* figures; they come directly from the federal investigators responsible for auditing the programs. Do you still believe that federal spending can't be cut—and cut drastically?

A few months ago, Ralph K. Winter, professor of law at Yale University, calculated that the increase in social welfare spending by local, state, and federal governments between 1960 and 1971, if given directly to poor people in America, would have provided the average family with an annual income of $19,000! Why did they in fact actually receive less than half that amount? Because the bureaucrats kept the rest to run the programs!

Writing in the American Enterprise Institute's *Regulation,* Professor Winter reported: "We can, in fact, eliminate poverty, reduce taxes and inflation, and limit the size of government by giving only some of the money already devoted to social welfare directly to the poor and leaving the rest with the taxpayer." But that, of course, would leave the bureaucratic middlemen out of the picture. And you can be sure they're not about to support any sensible procedure that might abolish their departments. Why, some of them might have to go to *work* if that happened!

When President Carter took office in January 1976, he knew his administration faced huge problems with the "welfare mess." So many workers had gone on the dole during the recession of 1974-75 that 31 states had run out of unemployment funds. An outraged populace expected the new administration to do "something." The word from the White House was "streamline."

Shortly thereafter, the game plan was announced:

Welfare programs in 1977 would cost "only" $2.8 billion more than the structure left over from the Nixon-Ford era (when Republicans had vowed to "do something"). Even the $2.8 billion was a jump from Carter's promise to have a welfare program no bigger than the one in effect in 1976, but by 1977, nobody thought a $2.8 billion overrun was exorbitant.

Digging by Capitol Hill welfare experts who looked closely at "reform" proposals to put as many as 50 million Americans on welfare found the "streamlining" would cost, not $2.8 billion more, but $15 billion more. Such notables as former U.S. Welfare Commissioner Robert Carlson charged that HEW played statistical games to downplay the projected splurge in welfare spending.

In truth, the Carter Administration is *not* any closer to cleaning up "the welfare mess" than was any of its predecessors. But it won't admit it.

All of this massive spending is in the good name of "eliminating poverty" and "creating jobs." There is virtually no effort to get *taxpayers* out of the squeeze Big Brother has put them in.

The Tax Foundation reported in 1977 that the average American earns $15,000 a year, is married, and is the father of two children. In 1977, he paid $3,975 in federal taxes—$1,459 in individual income tax, $878 in Social Security, and $1,635 in indirect federal taxes. A third of the overall amount, or $1,288, went to social programs, with $934 to national defense. On top of that, of course, our average Joe paid $365 for health expenditures and $353 in interest on the national debt.

Joe probably believes that this weekly debit from his paycheck is filtering down through the waves of advisers, social workers, counselors, caseworkers, urban renewal experts, planners, consultants, grantwriters, budget-drafters, and assorted other hangers-on to "the poor."

And some of it is, by golly. But the hard fact is that the cost of getting it where it is supposed to go is geometrically multiplied when it is done through Washington. The Association of Life Underwriters estimated in early 1977 that for every dollar reaching the needy, the cost of channeling it through churches is 8 cents; through charitable organizations, 27 cents—and to get one dollar through the government, it costs $3.00!

Nowhere has the largesse of welfare been more generous than New York City, the first "federalized" metropolis in America. Some $4 billion in welfare funds are targeted for New York City annually.

The Big Apple is the city where one out of every eight people survives on the dole—call it "welfare," "relief," or what-have-you. The city is positively papered with food stamps. Apparently it is also riddled with disease, if the large numbers of applicants for Medicaid mean anything.

A study by the Rand Corporation two years ago showed that a majority of New York's "welfare families" received cash, goods, and services that lifted 80 to 90 percent of them above the "poverty line"—whatever that really is. The Rand researchers found the average family on welfare in 1974 received the equivalent of $6,595 in cash, goods and services—or $1,595 above the then-established $5,000 "poverty level."

So varied are the programs available, and so generous are the administrators in New York City, that a typical welfare recipient is paid more than twice as much in benefits as the same person would get in Cleveland, and almost three times what he would get in Houston.

The federally financed Rand study helped answer the one important question about New York City welfare: Why do so many people work to get *on* the city's welfare rolls, but so few work to get off them? The answer is, you live better—and easier—*on* welfare!

Los Angeles was a step behind New York in jumping on the give-away bandwagon, but by 1977 it had surpassed Gotham, when more than a million Angelenos (or one in *seven*) were welfare recipients. Hovering near the 1-in-8 ratio are St. Louis, Baltimore, Washington, D.C., and Philadelphia.

The history of the welfare mess is not encouraging to those taxpayers hoping for some relief. Aid to Families with Dependent Children was enacted in 1935 as the first of the big welfare programs (excluding Social Security). Supplemental Security Income was enacted in 1972 to aid the aged, blind and disabled, and is the only major program providing direct cash assistance. Medicaid, food stamps, and housing subsidies are specific-need programs which are so broad and so costly they are virtually separate welfare programs in and of themselves.

The benefit levels under AFDC swing violently, from a low of $60 per month in Mississippi to a high of $497 per month in Hawaii. A recent study of five major welfare programs showed that benefits ranged from $370 per "poor" individual in Wyoming to more than $3,000 in Hawaii. In the Northeast, benefits are three times those available in the South.

In 23 states, the red tape involved in Aid to Families with Dependent Children actually encourages families to break up, because such states deny AFDC payments to poor families with unemployed fathers living at home. And the regulations even reward unemployment—should a poor mother earn just enough to lose her AFDC eligibility, she also may lose her eligibility for Medicaid, which may be worth anywhere from hundreds to thousands of dollars per year for her family.

If the head of an AFDC household does return to work, benefits to the family are not normally ended as soon as the job starts; they are phased out. Last year it was reported that in Michigan an AFDC family of four with a mother employed at $7,000 a year continued to draw more than $1,200 in cash benefits, plus Medicaid *and* $300 worth of food stamps each month. But a two-parent family of four in the same state, with a father working *at the same wage,* received no assistance!

And as for food stamps, this other well-intentioned program has been so susceptible to fraud and abuse it is even *more* out of control! The food stamp operation costs between $5 and $6 billion each year, with one out of every eleven Americans now getting stamps. Such problems as theft, illegal trafficking, counterfeiting, and fraudulent uses cost millions of dollars a year. The U.S. Department of Agriculture, which administers the program, has had to devote a quarter of its criminal investigative efforts into sorting through the mess.

Last year, U.S.D.A. reported that 83,016 people falsified applications for food stamps in 1976. A majority of the abuses involve purchases other than food with the stamps, reselling stamps for cash, and the like. "With food stamps you can buy anything out in the street, from booze to a prostitute to drugs," said an agent of the Ramsey County Welfare Fraud Unit in St. Paul, Minnesota.

A Grand Jury in Atlanta earlier this year confirmed that food stamps had been used to buy heroin, cocaine, and marijuana; thousands of dollars worth of beer and whiskey; televisions, stereos, records, and tapes; a fun time at a local massage parlor; and even a brand-new Cadillac! No one in law enforcement seemed the least bit surprised at the abuses that were uncovered. No one in the welfare agencies seemed to care. And the leader of the local "welfare rights" organization screamed that she was sick and tired of seeing "poor people" picked upon by the Establishment. "It's time we were treated with a little respect," she demanded.

A Secret Service official said $306,049 in bogus food stamps were seized in 1976, but that there is no real way to tell how many are in circulation because the Federal Reserve spot-checks only two percent of collected stamps once every six business days.

Clearly, a huge portion of the food stamp give-away results in fraud and worse. Error is another factor. A U.S.D.A spokesman reported early this year that "some kind of error" is involved in from 20 to 30 percent of all food stamp cases. In 1977 alone, these errors resulted in $590 million in benefits for people who either were ineligible or who received overpayments.

In 1965, when the food stamp program was in diapers, $35.1 million was targeted so that 442,359 persons who fell into specific "poverty" categories could receive reductions in their overall food bills by presenting the coupons. Caseloads exploded so rapidly that by 1977 the tab was around $6 billion, with 18 million Americans on the receiving end. Either Americans had gotten poorer, or the definition of poverty had changed, or the program was not working.

Poorer? Hardly. By 1976, federal officials pointed out that six percent of the current recipients of food stamps (1,140,000 families) had family incomes above $9,000. Some three percent (570,000 families) had incomes above $12,000. That was the year Senator Jesse Helms pointed out that "fifty-seven percent of those eligible are above the federal government's official poverty line."

How on earth is that possible? The eligibility formula is so loosely structured, and so susceptible of manipulation, that four-member families with incomes up to $12,000 qualify for the stamps. Involved in the formula are deductions of expenses for income taxes, retirement, Social Security, union dues, medical costs, child care, private school tuition, car payments, and up to a half of housing costs. Under this formula, it actually helps to own an expensive home with high mortgage payments!

If there are really not that many Americans truly in need of food stamps, can we really believe that unemployment—that other big bugaboo of the welfare state—is as bad as the generous dispensers of tax monies make out?

Since 1977, the federal government's Comprehensive Employment and Training Act (CETA) has spent more than $8 billion in an effort to help the nation's unemployed. Indeed, more than 750,000 people have been added to the public payroll in what amounts to make-work jobs.

But CETA is also loaded with fraud, theft and embezzlement. Newspaper accounts of criminal abuse in CETA have uncovered scandals from Maine to Miami, from New York to Honolulu. In fact, it is a *rare* CETA program where someone's hand has not been found raiding the goodie jar. Yet Congress recently approved a staggering $46 *billion* in additional funds for the program! Honesty may be mighty scarce at CETA— but apparently the welfare votes are mighty plentiful.

Columnist Paul Harvey, researching the "unemployment" quagmire last year, found that money taken from productive Americans and given to the unproductive now totals $200 billion a year. It is one reason, he said, why the number of American men who actually can work, but don't want to, has jumped 71 percent in nine years—and why "help wanted" lineage in newspapers increased during 27 out of the 28 months that he checked them.

A recent survey by Fordham University revealed that millions of young Americans would rather take welfare or other government handouts than do honest, if menial, work. "Our study revealed that the younger the person, the more likely he or she is to feel they would rather take government assistance or welfare than work at a menial job," the survey reported. "We think this attitude toward work is, in part, tied to the general affluence in our society. Today a person does not need to work in order to survive." The report concluded that between a quarter and a third of those who are not working are unemployed *because they choose to be*.

These individuals only want "meaningful" work, or work which gives them pleasure, and in their scale of values, being on the federal take while available jobs go begging is not immoral or unethical.

There are now welfare dynasties in America— families that have spent decades on welfare and the dole. Of the 3.4 million American families on welfare in 1975, more than 35 percent had been on the take five years or longer, and some 71,326 had been on relief for 20 years or more.

As Professor Nathan Glazer of Harvard University notes:

> *We have legitimized a level of welfare support ... which, on the whole, is greater than the support ...*

from the low-wage labor market. A lot of humani-
tarians say that reducing welfare means more suf-
fering for some people. I suppose that's true. But I
think it's also true that if we make welfare harder to
get, a lot of people will do other things—go to work,
for example.

Amen!

In 1976, the average New York City taxpayer paid
$159 to support the city's welfare system. The average
Chicagoan was taxed $170, the average Detroiter
kicked in $222. But in Houston, Texas, the average
citizen was taxed a mere $15.93 to support welfare
there.

The Good Life simply isn't available for welfare users
in the Lone Star state. While in many states, as we
have seen, welfare pays better than working, not so in
Texas. There the top payment a family of four can
expect is $140 a month.

Before you throw your hands up in horror at those
heartless Texans, consider this: Texas' unemployment
remains less than the national average. More impor-
tantly, while New York City welfare-drawers stay on
the dole an average of 34 months, Texans do so for 11.
And unlike anywhere else, 40 percent of Texans leave
welfare to take a job.

Many Texans also have a sense of humor about the
frustration of dealing with Big Brother. The City of
Hondo, Texas, was seeking $700,000 in federal aid for a
new civic center. But it was advised that its miniscule
three-percent unemployment rate disqualified it for
such funds. Well-managed cities without major problems are not allowed on the gravy train—even though
they help pay for it.

Mayor Woodrow Glasscock, Jr., needed to raise Hondo's unemployment rate to six percent, to bring it within the federal requirements. Rather than encourage anyone to quit a job, however, or laying off any city workers, he advertised for: "bums, loafers, and ne'er-do-wells; you're welcome in Hondo..." As of this writing, we don't know if enough bums arrived in Hondo to meet the wishes of Uncle Sam.

Please excuse me for that moment of levity. By and large, it's hard to maintain any sense of humor, when the terrible toll of the present welfare system is considered. We share the anguish and the outrage of one mother in Boston, who sent the following letter to *Human Events* magazine a few weeks ago:

> *Recently I read an editorial about poor people. I became so enraged that I almost wept. It was the kind of dribble that is perpetuating the myth of poverty in this country.*
>
> *I know that thousands, maybe hundreds of thousands, of poor people read it too, but with rapt expressions on their faces. Why should they even attempt to overcome something that gets such good press?*
>
> *It is common knowledge that self-pity is a destroying thing. How is is that pity somehow becomes noble when it comes from somebody else? The same people who wouldn't give a drink to an alcoholic or a fix to a junkie, think nothing of giving pity to the poor.*

She makes some awfully good points. But she didn't stop there. How many times have you seen a newspaper story, magazine article, or television report that riles your blood like this:

I become enraged when I see on television ruined buildings, garbage and rats in housing projects and other low-income dwellings. I become even more enraged when I see officials slobbering all over the terrible living conditions of those poor people.

Who do they think is causing those terrible living conditions? Who do they think is tearing those buildings apart? Who do they think is throwing the garbage out to feed the rats?

...The chiseling and cheating is so pervasive, it's like an inalienable right. So much misery is created by people who spend their lives living lies. They blame all their problems on a lack of money and it just isn't so. It's a lack of morality, masquerading as a lack of money. If they put half the effort into honestly trying to solve their real problems, as they do into dishonest chasing or chiseling money, they would have a chance at happiness.

We've got to stop giving poverty such a good name. It's something that should be overcome; not worn like a badge of merit.

But perhaps the most incredible truth of all is that, for all intents and purposes, poverty *has* been abolished in this country! The Census Bureau, official tabulator of U.S. statistics, does not agree with this, of course. According to their latest figures, approximately twelve percent of our population, or 26 million Americans, live below the officially defined "poverty" level. But very few of these people would be considered "poor" in any other nation of the world.

Dr. Martin Anderson of the Hoover Institution at Stanford University analyzed the Census Bureau computations and found that, in actual fact, less than thirty percent of the Census Bureau totals live in actual "poverty." Professor George A. Levitan of George Washington University goes even further: "If poverty is a lack of basic needs," he says, "we have almost eliminated poverty in the United States."

Columnist M. Stanton Evans puts his finger on a major part of the problem when he reports, "Poverty *per se,* in short, has all but been abolished. The official change most urgently needed is not in further payouts from HEW, but in more realistic bookkeeping from the Bureau of the Census."

The truth is even more simple. The most urgent need in solving the poverty mess is to get the federal government out of the poverty business. Give the states, local communities, and voluntary agencies the responsibility for meeting the needs of their citizens. And at the same time, let their citizens keep more of their earnings, let local government get its fair share of taxes, and the "poverty mess" will disappear almost overnight. As a farmer friend of mine puts it, "The only way to trim the fat is to put a fence between the hogs and the trough."

That is *exactly* what must be done by us taxpayers. We need to bind the hands of the Big Spenders in Washington the same way they were handcuffed in California—by law. The vast majority of politicians and bureaucrats will never take their hands out of our pockets voluntarily. Let them determine your neighbor's needs, and your ability to pay, and the robbery will just get worse.

It's time to start putting up some fences!

Chapter Six
Big Brother's Bureaucrats

In 1977, Montgomery County, Maryland coffee shop owner Jim Jordan grew increasingly frustrated over a sea of red tape and regulations that had kept him from opening his new business. As he saw his dream of a lifetime—owning and operating his own business—going down the drain, he begged and pleaded and fought, until he just couldn't take it anymore. He committed suicide.

Jordan had taken over a rundown sandwich shop and planned to turn it into a family restaurant. Entrepreneurial spunk? You bet. But....

First, his kitchen was closed down for three months while an inspector filed a report on a minor violation. Then the county's environmental protection agency forced him to change his doorway (cost: $4,000), and fire marshals made him change it again (second cost: $3,000). He received constantly changing rulings on his application for a liquor license.

"Every time Jim turned around he was hit by such problems," his attorney said. "It broke him in the end."

Jim Jordan's death was a particularly tragic result of the problems Americans face from the bureaucracy created to "protect" them. But in thousands of less dramatic ways, millions of us feel his frustration. We know that government regulations are binding us just as securely as the Lilliputians bound Gulliver to the beach. And it's happening the same way—one thread at a time.

Some of the intrusions into our lives by government would seem almost funny—if the net result of all the assaults by the regulators weren't so tragic for our nation.

Last year, for example, the Department of Health, Education and Welfare made the shocking discovery that there was an all-boy choir operating in the elementary schools of Wethersfield, Connecticut. Maintaining a choir of boy sopranos was "sex discrimination," said HEW. The school officials were told they would lose their $70,000 annual windfall in federal funds unless girls sang along. The choir was abandoned. Notch one up for HEW.

Earlier this year, the zealous sexists at HEW said Title XI of the Education Amendments of 1972 (which require that no person "shall on the basis of sex be excluded from participation in, be denied the benefits of, or be subject to discrimination under any educational program or activity receiving federal financial assistance") was not being properly enforced. Singling out *cheerleaders* in Oak Ridge, Tennessee, those overpaid, underworked minions of the bureaucracy interpreted Title XI to mean that forthwith "it ... will be necessary that varsity cheerleaders cheer equally for both boys' and girls' varsity teams." The only surprise is that they didn't send a planeload of inspectors to every ball game to measure the volume of cheers at every match!

But this was just the beginning. HEW also proclaimed that if Oak Ridge was to have cheerleaders at all, there must be an "affirmative action" recruitment of males. Having just girls as cheerleaders reinforces the "stereotypical supportive roles of females," don't you know, and the Big Uncle can't permit that. The snoopers from HEW also found another danger to the

Republic in Tennessee's high schools: Unless girls start playing basketball by the same rules as boys, they warned, all of their federal money would be shut off.

The Department of Health, Education and Welfare is undoubtedly the most bloated bureaucracy in Washington. It is nothing less than a despotic gang that is empowered to pry into virtually every aspect of your life and make sure you realize just how you fit into the collective scheme of things. It was one of Jimmy Carter's favorite targets as he sought votes riding the wave of popular disgust over big government.

Just as Ford, Nixon, Johnson, and everyone before him, Carter had promised to "do something" about the size and grasp of government. Appointing Cabinet members who were committed to fiscal integrity was supposed to be part of the new look. At HEW, Joseph Califano quickly showed the entrenched bureaucrats they had nothing to worry about.

In one of his first actions, "Joltin' Joe" quietly sneaked his personal cook onto the public payroll as a "personal assistant." By mid-1977, his personal assistant even had an assistant—to wait on the Big Boss's table!

Well-known cost-cutter Michael Blumenthal, Secretary of the Treasury, maintains a personal chef and dining room (the chef gets $12,000 a year) while Commerce Secretary Juanita Kreps brought in a $15,000-a-year private chef who cooks *only* for Juanita, and then only on special occasions. Labor Secretary F. Ray Marshall's private cook cost taxpayers $14,900 this year. Attorney General Griffin Bell, apparently a White House gourmand, has not one but *two* personal cooks (at $18,194 and $14,038 annually), plus four busboys who get nearly $250 a week for cleaning up.

Transportation Secretary Brock Adams "borrowed"

four U.S. Coast Guardsmen to do the culinary duties around his pad. But none of these "fiscally responsible" Cabinet members can hold a brandy snifter to Defense Secretary Harold Brown, for whom taxpayers have graciously retained nineteen enlisted men and one civilian at an annual tab of $173,232 to feed him and 117 top Pentagon brass.

Dr. Larry McDonald, a Congressman from the President's home state of Georgia, commented acidly: "If this is supposed to be an example of government 'without frills,' I'd hate to see what would happen if these gentlemen suddenly decided to live high on the hog!" Such lavish living makes as much sense as the 124 people who hold jobs operating U.S. Capitol elevators. Their average annual salary is $8,600, which doesn't sound too bad—until you learn that every elevator is automatic!

Everywhere you look in Washington you will find bloated staffs, soft jobs, and bureaucrats who have built small empires for themselves. There simply is no feasible way to describe the enormity of Washington's bureaucracy, or its true cost to American taxpayers. The following figures will give you some idea, however, of the Big Brother behemoth.

As of 1978, for the first time in our history, the number of persons supported by the federal government surpassed the number working for private enterprise. There are now 71,900,000 Americans working to pay the tab for 88,200,000 persons receiving checks each month from Uncle Sam.

The total number of civilian employees on federal, state and local payrolls is more than triple what it was 25 years ago. There is now one "public servant" for every 4.5 workers in the private sector. The cost of maintaining this spiraling bureaucracy is an incredible 886 percent higher than the bill in 1950, and the end is nowhere in sight. Governmental salaries for civilians alone were a startling $152.6 *billion* in 1975, as contrasted to $12.7 billion in 1950.

As just one example of the padded salaries for federal bureaucrats, consider the tremendous "sacrifices" being made by leaders of the so-called "war on poverty." The head of ACTION, 34-year-old former anti-Vietnam activist Sam Brown, pulls down a cool $52,000 a year for his efforts, and just bought a plush, $160,000 house on Washington's Embassy Row. His deputy is Mary King, wife of Carter's ex-drug advisor Peter Bourne. Her take? Another $50,000 a year. She and her husband live in a $171,000 Washington showplace—far beyond the standards and life styles that most of us who pay their salaries ever dream of achieving. Margery Tabankin earns $42,000 a year for running VISTA. The acronym stands for *Volunteers* In Service To America. But you won't catch Ms. Tabankin volunteering to work for a paltry $20,000 or $30,000 a year! And on and on it goes. There are a lot of people having the time of their life—and enjoying the pay and perks of their life—spending your money to fight poverty! Who says poverty doesn't pay?

The federal government owns one-third of all land in this country (760 million acres). Plus title to 405,000 buildings at a cost of $91 billion. But even this isn't enough; $663 million is spent annually for rent on another 54,000 structures. This is an empire that Caesar or Charlemagne would have envied!

Bureaucrats administer 1,040 separate domestic programs and dispense or deal with more than 4,500 official forms. The paperwork alone would fill the Washington Monument eleven times per year! To handle the flood of paper, the federal government employs 211,000 secretaries, typists, and clerks. The cost to us who foot the bills is a staggering $140 billion per year!

Is all of this necessary because of all of the new laws Congress passes each year? Hardly! In a good year (or bad, depending on your point of view) Congress approves about 500 laws. But federal departments and agencies promulgate that many new regulations *every week!* That is 25,000 new rules—with the effect of law—every year. Even more frightening, hundreds of thousands of interpretations of these regulations pour forth every year. Is it any wonder that businessmen say they are drowning in a sea of red tape?

Congressman Gene Snyder is hardly exaggerating when he points out:

> *Mushrooming government runs our lives more and more. Regulations bind our activites, our children's education, and our enterprise tighter each year. We heat, light, and cool our homes, and power our plants with regulated power. We move ourselves and our freight on regulated roads, buses, trucks and airlines. We're told what we can build and where to build it....Businesses are told whom they can hire and how much they must pay, how they can advertise, and a million other things requiring tons of paperwork and hundreds of thousands of man-hours to complete.*
>
> *If you break a law, you are supposed to be considered innocent until the state proves you guilty. But if you violate a regulation, you are guilty as charged unless you can prove your innocence to the bureaucrats who wrote it. When you go to a hearing at your expense, they act as prosecution, judge, jury, and executioner,* and you pay their salaries.

The cost of all this regulation, according to the Office of Management and Budget, is about $140 billion each and every year. That is, it would take 140,000 men, each carrying a million dollars, to transport the cash necessary to pay for a single year of federal regulation.

At the Internal Revenue Service, regulation and implementation mean that IRS forms for a single year, if stacked, would be *two miles high*. Federal regulation means ten billion sheets of paper churned out annually by the Government Printing Office—a rate that would fill fifty major league football stadiums. Why aren't environmental extremists screaming about the forests of innocent trees which must give their lives to be turned into forms for bureaucrats?

Harvard University employs twenty-six people, at an annual cost of $300,000, simply to prepare all of the reports required by the government for all of the federal grants it receives!

Over at the Food and Drug Administration, it now takes up to 200,000 pieces of paper, anywhere from five to ten years, and a cost of $14 to $20 million, to license a new anesthetic.

Virtually every new administration during the past twenty years has made *some* effort to halt the paper deluge. For example, in late 1975, Gerald Ford issued an order to cut all paperwork by ten percent. At that time, it was taking Americans 134.9 million hours to complete 453.3 million responses on 5,148 different federal forms.

A year later, the *number* of federal forms had been reduced to 4,504—a 12½ percent drop. Yet it was taking Americans 138.5 million hours to complete 407 million responses. Total man-hours went up 36 million hours! Why? The crafty bureaucrats had simply added more questions to many of the forms they retained.

We've all heard the argument that our population is bigger and things are more complicated. But this hardly accounts for the fact that, although our population has grown 60 times larger since 1789, our bureaucracy has multiplied 8,170 times!

Between 1952 and 1972, the public payroll multiplied more than fourfold, from $35 to $150 billion. At the same time, total wages and salaries in the private sector grew only 247 percent. During those same two decades, the number of public employees grew by 52 percent, those in the private sector only 35 percent. Average annual earnings advanced 183 percent in government, a lower 146 percent in private industry.

The National Taxpayers Union was on the money, so to speak, with its brochure titled, "Politicians and Bureaucrats came to Washington to do good...and they have done very well." For example:

The average federal employee gets fifty percent more paid time off than a person working in the private sector. He gets *many* more automatic pay raises. Governmental employees earn more than their counterparts in the private sector by the time they retire. And their pensions are designed to rise automatically faster than the rate of inflation.

Right now, there are more than 32,000 federal workers getting $40,000 or more a year. Half of these well-paid bureaucrats are stationed in Washington, a "blue chip" city where one out of five workers makes $30,000 or more a year!

During the 1976 Presidential campaign, Jimmy Carter said: "Our Government in Washington now is a horrible bureaucratic mess. We must give top priority to a drastic and thorough reorganization of the federal bureaucracy." A year after his inauguration, however, federal employees had *increased* by several thousand new bureaucrats. Why? *U.S. News and World Report* described part of the problem:

> *At the peak of the bureaucratic pile, just below those appointed by the new President to top-level jobs, are the supermanagers who make the system work or not work. These managers can speed or delay action, sometimes irrespective of policies laid down by the President. They can sidetrack or promote bills in Congress where they have forged close-working ties that transcend party lines. In short, top career bureaucrats can make a shambles of Government reorganization plans that threaten their corners of the federal world.*

There are empires in Washington—and even empires within empires. A career employee at Housing and Urban Development spoke for many of the entrenched bureaucrats when he said:

> *Assistant secretaries are appointed by the Secretary. They bring their own favorites, some political, some just friends. There's a ripple effect all the way down. The civil-service system doesn't work to protect jobs of the qualified—it just keeps you from being outright fired. They can always put you in the basement.*

In a structure that operates without competition, without fiscal restraint, with no real accountability, no need to be efficient, no danger of being fired, and a virtually unlimited source of revenue—you and me—nobody is going to cut a budget, fire a buddy, or shake the system.

How many federal employees like Jubal Hale are

there hidden away somewhere in Washington? He is a government lawyer who admits he has *no work* to do for his $20,000 annual salary. He spends about eight hours a day reading books and listening to Beethoven symphonies.

Hale was hired in 1971 as executive secretary of the recently created Federal Metal and Non-Metallic Mine Safety Board of Review. Never hear of the outfit? Neither had I. It was launched in 1970 with a modest $167,000 Congressional appropriation. Hale's job was to listen to appeals from mine operators who had run afoul of safety regulations. However, his office never received a single complaint! The Office of Management and Budget was notified of the situation, but decided it was easier to continue the appropriations than to go through all the fuss and bother of trying to abolish a federal review board!

Carl Carlson is a "special assistant to a regional postmaster general" who earns $37,000 per year. Last year he confessed: "I come to work about 8:30, and I read the paper for awhile. I get some coffee. Then I go to lunch. I may read a magazine. I get certain clippings from a clipping service, and I read them. I get a daily labor report, and I read that. Then it's probably five o'clock, and it's time to go home. If I didn't have a sense of humor, I would have been put away a long time ago."

Carlson was forced out of a responsible position in September 1975, because his supervisor wanted someone else. "I just wasn't one of his cronies," Carlson explains. As of October 1977, this federal employee had been reporting to an unused storeroom in Philadelphia for over two years. He was doing virtually nothing, but getting paid $37,000 a year to do it!

Martin Judge, magazine editor for a federal publication, describes it this way:

Government is the one place where the Peter Principle—the idea that one rises to his level of incompetence—doesn't work. In government you can rise far, far beyond it.

A former researcher at the Library of Congress (who asked for a transfer to another agency because she didn't have any work to do), observed:

At the Library, it's obvious people are sitting around not doing anything. For Pete's sake, I wrote my master's paper while I was there. It was a common thing. Yet when it was budget time, all people talked about was hiring more bodies just to get new slots for the office. That's the big bureaucratic game: Get as many positions as you can, even though you don't need them, because you succeed in government if you have lots of people working for you.

A civilian worker at the Military Traffic Management Command reports that his section has five people earning $20,000 per year, doing unnecessary work.

Some employees have attempted to blow the whistle on lazy, idle, corrupt, or incompetent employees. But as Senator Patrick J. Leahy reported last year, more often than not, the cost-conscious, responsible bureaucrats who point out errors, omissions, and waste in their departments are branded as troublemakers. They are fired or frozen out of their promotions:

• Dr. Anthony Morris, an employee of the National Institute of Health, was convinced that flu vaccines were ineffective and sometimes dangerous. He was transferred to the Food and Drug Administration. When the government announced the big Swine Flu

Innoculation Program, with President Ford's personal endorsement televised nationally, Dr. Morris tried to stop the program. He was fired from the FDA for "insubordination and inefficiency." But a few months later, the swine-flu program, one of Washington's more spectacular bungles, was quietly terminated when numerous fatalities occurred among those who had lined up to get their shots.

• Two U.S. Indian Health Service nurses at Shiprock, New Mexico, dared go to Congress and the press with evidence of unsanitary conditions and lack of proper staffing at the hospital. Both were fired.

• Robert Tucker and Robert F. Sullivan of the General Services Administration were summarily fired when they revealed that millions of dollars in contracts between GSA and local builders had been falsely classified as "emergencies," thus eliminating the need for competitive bidding.

• Pity the plight of Ralph Applegate, who made price evaluations on small-item purchases for the Defense Construction Supply Center at Columbus, Ohio. He discovered that his supervisor often preferred certain suppliers, whose prices were far in excess of reasonable market costs. Applegate went to his superiors, then complained to a Congressional committee, and then to the U.S. Controller General's Office. First, he was suspended. He received his first "unsatisfactory performance" rating in 15 years of service. When he took his case to the press, he was fired for insubordination.

During the recent investigation of the multi-million dollar rip-offs in the General Services Administration, Senator Sam Nunn of Georgia had the following exchange with William Clinkscales, who is Chief of Investigations for GSA:

Doesn't it seem that with all this white collar crime that the only people who really get punished are the whistle-blowers — the ones who really do a good job?

Clinkscales reply was short and almost painfully honest. "Yes, it does," he mumbled. And remember, this is the man who was *Chief of Investigations* for the entire agency. Why isn't corruption in government eliminated? Because most bureaucrats, who honestly want fair and honest administration, know that sticking their neck out is probably the *only* way they could lose their job! The bloated bureaucracy protects its own. If one incompetent or dishonest employee can be fired, why, anyone's job might be next.

Such blatant cover-ups and protection of wrong-doing are not limited to the federal government, by any means. It goes on in *any* bureaucracy. The bigger the state structure, the worse the abuses. Find a government agency which, at year's end, *returns* taxpayer funds with a request for a smaller budget, and you will have arrived in taxpayers' Heaven.

With well-paid bureaucrats protected from their errors, waiting to collect the pension gold at the end of the taxpayer-provided rainbow, sloppiness, poor planning, and rampant waste are sure to occur. And here again, the totals are mind-boggling.

In 1977 alone, cost overruns on federal projects amounted to $201.5 billion. That is 72 percent more than the original estimated costs, and $125 billion more than the previous year's overruns. Such "errors" are a chronic problem in Washington. The chief offender in 1977 was the Department of Transportation, whose projects ran an incredible $70 billion above estimates. Defense ran a close second, with overruns of $62.5 billion.

The General Accounting Office, which compiled these figures, based its report on 808 civil and military projects that were expected to cost $281 billion but in fact are costing taxpayers $482 billion. The Army Corps of Engineers holds the single-project record—its 1964 estimate that a hurricane protection project in Louisiana would cost $10.8 million has been revised upward to $138 million—a 1,178% hike! The U.S. Coast Guard's 336% overrun on the cost of surveillance aircraft (current estimate: $363.1 million, vs. an initial figure of $83.3 million) seems almost reasonable by comparison.

The Air Force planned to build a fleet of F-15 fighters in 1969 for $6.04 billion. Seven years later, the price had soared to $12.17 billion. The Navy's Trident submarine and missile development program was announced in 1974 with a $12.4 billion price tag. By 1976 it was $18.85 billion. The Army's XM-1 tank was to cost $3 billion when the program was announced in 1972; the cost had gone to $4.9 billion four years later. And on and on it goes.

But what about programs and projects where waste, like beauty, is in the eyes of the beholder? How about such vital endeavors as "research" grants for $500,000 to determine why humans and monkeys sometimes clench their teeth? Or $40,000 to find out why spiders build webs where insects can be found? (The report bears the title, "Spider Distribution Associated with Prey Density.") Or $81,000 to explore the social behavior of the Alaskan brown bear? Or a modest $36,500 study on the "Evolution of Song Learning of Parasitic Finches"? A book the size of the Los Angeles yellow pages could be filled with similar examples.

Of the 226 million square feet of building space which our government owns, an incredible 15 million square feet (equal to 250 skyscrapers, each 60 stories tall) are now vacant. Acquiring this excess property cost taxpayers more than $2 billion, the General Accounting Office reports. Last year, the GAO found $6.2 million worth of waste in leases and $19.5 million worth of waste in construction in just four cities: Los Angeles, San Francisco, New Orleans, and Honolulu.

The federal government is not only the largest owner *and renter* of office space in America, it is also the largest home and apartment owner in the world.

Just three years ago, public records revealed that the Department of Housing and Urban Development owned 277,000 *vacant* apartment units and 57,000 *vacant* single-family homes. HUD spokesman Donald Hall admitted: "HUD did make mistakes, many mistakes. We got into a push for production that was just too much for us to handle. Quality fell way down, and we had a lot of inexperienced people in jobs all across the country. And there was a lot of hanky-panky going on—bribes."

Most federal boondoggles had their genesis under previous administrations. But the newest Cabinet agency, the Department of Energy, is an inspiration of President Carter. Its budget for fiscal 1978 was $10.6 billion, to finance a staff of 19,767 people. This breaks down to $500,000 per employee—or $50 for each and every member of our total population of 212 million Americans. It represents $266,871 for each of the 39,763 wells drilled in 1976; $3.95 for each barrel of domestic crude oil produced in 1976; it exceeds the 1975 capital and exploration expenditures of the entire petroleum industry; and it is larger than all of the profits of the seven largest oil companies in 1974—profits which the anti-oil industry folks call "obscene."

In Washington, as elsewhere, there is plenty of disagreement over which agency is the most prudent and which the most wasteful; which is essential and which the most frivolous. But there is absolutely no doubt whatever which is the largest. In all realms of Big Brother, the biggest is the Department of Health, Education and Welfare.

HEW Secretary Joseph Califano presides over an empire that includes 1,125,000 employees. Its annual budget, now approaching $200 billion a year, is exceeded by only two other governmental structures on earth: the Soviet Union, and the *total* budget of the federal government. As *Time* magazine noted in its issue of June 12, 1978, HEW:

> *provides funds, advice and regulations for birth, infancy, up-bringing, schooling and old age, for the sick and disabled, the handicapped and the gifted, the divorced and the depressed, the sex discriminator and the sex offender, for those who are pregnant and for those who are sterile. Whatever the ailment or anxiety, the department will have some remedy among its 400 programs, a range of activities that increases so fast not even HEW's own top administrators can keep up with them all.*

Every day, HEW receives some 20,000 new claims from the put-upon, the put-down, and the put-away. Every night, it runs through some 220,000 reels of tape on its computers, to determine who should receive tomorrow's checks. Every hour the sun shines (and even when it rains), another $50 million is allocated by HEW for Medicaid, Medicare, Social Security, Head Start, aid to education, Public Health Service, student loans, the Food and Drug Administration, disability insurance, and about 1,600 other federal projects. Its electronic wizardry makes James Bond look as sophisticated as a bush man with a spear. It records so much information on so many citizens that more than a few of us sometimes wonder if 1984 has not already arrived.

So gigantic is Health, Education and Welfare, in fact, that in 1977 it *lost* $7 billion dollars, and didn't even miss it! This is the equivalent of *all* federal income taxes paid by four million families in this country! It is enough money to buy over one million luxury automobiles. And yet, it represents only *five percent* of HEW's budget for the year!

Recently, someone in HEW wanted to know how many consultants from private industry are also employed, on a part-time basis, by the department. Rockwell International was hired, for $348,147, to learn the answer. Months later, Rockwell researchers were still plowing through files and records—and had incurred "cost overruns" on its contract that totaled $2.2 million.

HEW's growth has been so explosive that it makes Jack's beanstalk seem puny by comparison. It all started in 1954, with a modest $5.4 billion appropriation under President Dwight Eisenhower. And $3.4 billion of that amount, or 60 percent, was for Social Security. Its 1978 budget is a gargantuan $182 billion—roughly 54 percent *more* than Congress appropriated last year for our entire defense and military-research needs. As *Time* magazine noted almost coyly:

Regardless of what party controls the White House, HEW has achieved a considerable measure of independence and a momentum that cannot be easily arrested.

Watching the price tag for various HEW-financed

programs shoot upward is enough to give you whiplash. Medicare and Medicaid payments went from $16.5 billion in 1974, to almost double that amount—an incredible $31.3 billion—just three short years later. Thanks in large part to the red tape involved in accepting all this money, the average cost of a hospital stay went zooming up for the rest of us as well: from $350 in 1965, to $1,300 in 1978, to an estimated $2,600 by 1983.

Another way to become instantly comfortable for life through HEW is disability insurance. The program cost working taxpayers an affordable $1.5 billion in 1965. This year, the price tag will be $13 billion. By 1985 it is expected to hit $27 billion. Why? Are we suddenly becoming a nation of the infirm? Not exactly.

As disability aid is extended to more and more categories (and it is virtually mandatory for bureaucrats to come up with at least *one* new area of expansion every year), it seems that more and more people who could return to work choose not to. "Disability" now covers anything from permanent paralysis to chronic headaches and a nervous tummy. So many people are lining up to get on this particular gravy train that HEW recently hired 650 more administrative judges, in an effort to weed through a backlog of almost 134,000 cases.

We have discussed Aid to Families with Dependent Children, food stamps, and other welfare programs in the previous chapter. But we should note here that under these programs, you and I spend $30 billion a year, to provide aid to some 30 million Americans. When HEW ran a partial computer check last year of the "needy" poor receiving this aid, the machines cranked out the names of 13,354 people currently employed by Uncle Sam in Washington—and another 12,980 who recently had left the federal work force.

Student loans are another example of federal largesse filled with indefensible abuses. In 1977, the default rate on such loans was sixteen percent. (The normal default rate for commercial loans is 2.5 percent or less.) You and I have paid over one billion dollars thus far to make good these loans. And interestingly enough, when the federal computers were turned on, to find out who had turned off their repayments, the names of 6,783 federal employees were discovered—including 317 people working for Health, Education and Welfare.

HEW is also the agency that recently increased its budget for anti-smoking "education" from $30 million to $85 million—while the Department of Agriculture increased its subsidies to the tobacco industry by almost the same amount. Wouldn't you think *someone* in Washington would ask, Why should money be taken from taxpayers to finance either part of this madness?

As Dr. Roger Freeman points out in *The Growth of American Government:*

> *We must recognize that, in contrast to private industry, where competition and the profit motive impose pressure for greater efficiency and a natural and generally reliable gauge of productivity, governmental programs have built-in counterproductive trends. It is a natural tendency for a public employee to want to handle fewer cases— pupils, tax returns, welfare families, crimes—in the belief that he could do a better job if he had a smaller workload, and most certainly have an easier life. For the supervisor there is a definite gain in stature, position—and even grade—by having a larger number of subordinates. This and the ideological commitments to the program goals and*

*methods of their professional fraternities provide a
powerful and well-nigh irresistible incentive for
empire building.*

There are thousands of volumes documenting the
waste and the rip-offs in the bloated, burgeoning federal bureaucracy. Many are on file in the offices of our
Congressmen. Shouldn't it be up to the representatives
of the people to do something about such incredible
extravagance?

Yes, it should be. And there is an increasing number
of fiscally-sound legislators in both houses. But so far
they are in a minority. For now, it is business as usual
in the halls of Congress, where the cost of their deliber-
ations is upwards of $800 million a year.

Can we expect fiscal restraint from Congress—the
same representatives of the people who voted themselves an inflation-proof salary increase in 1975, then
passed an additional salary increase in 1977, taking
them to $57,500 per year—all without the bother of a
debate? The same men and women who make the laws
which fuel inflation are now protected against its ravages, while we pay ... and pay ... and pay.

The cost of operating the Senate was $6 million in
1947. By 1976 it hit $137 million and was still climbing.
The number of Senate employees went from 1,710 in
1947 to 6,733 in 1976. No one is getting laid off there,
either.

The 1978 legislative budget called for $144.6 million
for the Senate and its committees; $262.3 million for the
House and its committees; $58.2 million for "services"
(joint committees, page boys, tour guides, medical
care); $9.8 million for the Congressional Budget Of-
fice; $125.6 million for construction and maintenance;
and $167.6 million for the General Accounting Office,
which is supposed to keep track of everything else.

Taxpayers also provide $16.8 million annually for the Capitol police force, now numbering about 1,100; $387,800 for Congress' very own medical staff; and $389,100 for the Capitol Guide Service, which used to provide guides for tourists at 25-cents per person, but now uses the subsidy to offer its services "free."

Each member of the House receives $255,144 as a "staff allowance;" the Senate staff allowance ranges up to $902,301. Senators also receive $5,000 for stationery; $1,740 for postage and franking of official mail; $2,200 plus the cost of 4,500 telephone calls; and the price of 44 round-trips home.

But wait, there's more. Each member of Congress receives $47,000 in life insurance policies for $36.14 per month and a pension to which they contribute eight percent of their salaries. The pension returns 2.5% of their salary for every year served. This allows ex-President Ford, for example, to collect $38,000 per year from this source alone. There are also special deals available for hospital care, furniture and supplies, free trips to garden spots around the world, expense-paid visits to Hawaii, Miami, and hundreds of other cities in this country, and much, much more.

In other words, it's a gravy train for the legislators, too. Most of them were elected on a platform that promised fiscal integrity, rolling back the cost of government, trimming the welfare rolls, and so on. But as a former President once expressed it, "To get along, go along." And most of our leaders learn to get along very, *very* well.

In 1958, Professor C. Northcote Parkinson calculated that if the rate of government growth in Britain continued at the present rate, everyone on the island would be working for the government by the year 2195.

In 1971, the Morgan Guaranty Trust Company

applied the same yardstick to the United States. It determined that if things continue here as they are now, everyone in this country will be on the public payroll by the year 2049—a century and a half earlier than in "socialized" Britain. It will never happen, of course. Long before we reach that point, the entire economy will come crashing down around our feet. Some people say they can already see the fissures and cracks. We simply *must* trim the bureaucracy — before it crushes us!

Chapter Seven
The Trillion-Dollar Ripoff

On December 20, 1977, President Carter presented the nation with "a Christmas present to Americans," as the media hyped it—Social Security "reforms" that will raise workers' taxes by $227 billion over the next ten years. HEW czar Joseph Califano hailed the measure as "an example of courageous and responsible government."

The presidential signature on the Social Security "reform" package followed by 19 months the presidential candidate's promise that, "I will never increase taxes for the working people of our country and the lower and middle income groups ... and you can depend on that if I am elected."

Of course, the new bite in 1978—a maximum of $1,087.85 per "contributor," up $105.52 over 1977—was considered modest. The giant jumps from this mass impoverishment of American taxpayers will not be felt until after 1978—deceitfully enough, *after* the Senators and Representatives who agreed to this outrage have been safely reelected.

In 1979, the maximum tax jumps another $400—or almost 40 percent!—as both the tax percentage goes up (from 5.85 to 6.1 percent) and the base is increased (from $17,700 to $22,900). But the fun is only starting. By 1987, the maximum Social Security taxable salary will jump to $42,600, with 7.15 percent of that, or a whopping $3,045.90 — going to Social Security alone. Lest that salary seem impossibly high to you, remember that with inflation it will be the equivalent of earning less than $18,000 a year now!

Taxes for the highest-paid workers will thus be *tripling* over the next ten years, as both the tax rate and the wage level on which it is based go up. And, of course, all other taxes—income, sales tax, *etc.,*—will also climb to the clouds.

What it all means is that by 1984, if your wages are $36,000—a projected modest income for that year due to inflation—you will be paying at least $2,500 annually, or over seven percent of your taxes, to Social Security alone. Your employer will be putting in a similar amount. (This will, of course, be in *addition* to what you will be paying in other taxes.) Since *you* also end up paying the employer's portion (all of his costs are passed on to consumers, in the form of higher prices), this means that a phenomenal *fourteen* percent of all salary and wages paid in this country will go toward financing the Social Security program. And it will still be bankrupt!

As economist Warren T. Brookes has warned in the *Boston Herald American*:

> *Congress and the President ... are combining to turn the little white lies on which Social Security was based into an enormous whopper so large that it could bring the whole economic house of cards we live in today crashing down around our collective ears. The added cost of this whopper to the American taxpayers, particularly at the middle and upper-income level, will come to more than $208 billion over the next 10 years, making it the largest tax increase in the nation's history—a tax increase that could cost this nation over 6 million lost jobs. Thus, instead of facing up to the inherent myths upon which the Social Security system has been*

*built, and rectifying them, they have chosen to go on
preserving these myths, at colossal cost to the
economy.*

Brookes wrote these lines *before* the "Christmas gift"
$227 billion law was signed into law a year ago. The
new tax levy on American workers means that, if you
spent a million dollars a day, it would take 625 *years* to
spend the additional tax revenue. The $227 billion
Social Security increase is roughly half of the entire
1978 federal budget. It is more than the entire federal
budget for 1971!

Even so, the Administration's announced goal of financial stability for the badly buffeted Social Security
system will not be attained. The new law simply means
much higher taxes, for a bigger tax extortion, to pay out
more "benefits," — which, by 1987, aren't apt to be
much more "beneficial" than they are today.

But since the amount employees pay is only half the
take — employers "contribute" the other half—it is
business, particularly small business, which in some
ways will be hit the most. Those skyrocketing "contributions" have already caused slowdowns in production, staff cutbacks and failure to expand. The hand-
writing on the wall for employers is clear: Hire fewer
people, install more labor-saving machines, and increase the price of the goods you produce. If you can't do
all of that, get ready for bankruptcy court.

Once again, Newspeak rears its linguistic head. In
the name of security for all, Big Brother will be providing poverty for the masses.

Ironically enough, as the Social Security tax bite
increases, the benefits will actually decline. While the
current system is supposed to provide a pension of
roughly 44 percent of a worker's earnings immediately

before his retirement, the new law will cut this amount to 41 percent by 1984.

Social Security, as a "system," has been officially bankrupt since at least 1975, when it took in $1.2 billion less than it paid out. It was $3.2 billion in the red in 1976, and $5.6 billion in hock in 1977. It was the extrapolation of these awful figures into the future that led the experts to realize that, unless something is done *fast,* the system would eventually be $17 *trillion* in the hole.

Last year, maximum benefits were about $460 per month. That figure is expected to rise slightly. But adjusting for an ever-more inflationary economy, the "benefits" come nowhere near the goal envisioned either by the original modest program or the multiple amendments to it that have been made in the past 41 years.

This is because the program—from its inception, through its changes, through the amendments, up to and including the new law—is a fraud.

It is a fraud that the legislators and implementers of Social Security have been very careful to have no part of. For the nation's seven million federal, state and local government employees can and do escape having to participate in the Social Security rip-off. The reason, of course, is that the federal insurance programs in which they are enrolled pay off a lot better than Social Security ever could, did or would—just as, we might add, can almost any private insurance plan.

It is upsetting in the extreme that government folks who peddle Social Security to the masses aren't about to settle for a Social Security check in their old age. They refuse to face life on the Social Security rolls at the end of a long career of guzzling at the public trough.

In 1977, Rep. Joseph L. Fisher, a Virginia Democrat

whose district covers a suburban area of Washington, D.C., which probably has more federal employees than any other congressional enclave in the nation, discovered that the most explosive issue among his constituents was preventing Congress from forcing federal workers to swap their own lucrative benefits for the Social Security "common folks" program.

At that time, under the Civil Service pension fund, federal employees contributed 7 percent of their pay (against Social Security's rate then of 5.85 percent), but received much better benefits. A $15,000-a-year government worker could retire after 30 years at $703 a month. A worker in private industry would labor for years longer, but receive 35 percent less—a paltry $460 per month.

Rep. Fisher soon found, as he worked on what he called his "greatest success," that teachers, firemen, sanitation workers, policemen, and other city, county, and state employees around the country were equally against being dragooned into the common-folks program. He was joined by such patricians as House Speaker Tip O'Neill, Ways and Means Chairman Al Ullman, and Post Office and Civil Service Chairman Robert N.C. Nix.

At length, as congressman after congressman was lobbied to oppose the great outrage of having such employees forced into the same system to which the rest of us must "contribute," the House overwhelmingly rejected the measure. It would, of course, have produced at least $25 billion for the bankrupt Social Security system in two years. In the meantime, we're all paying—through the income tax—more money than necessary to keep civil servants living in the Social Security-free retirement life to which they have become accustomed.

The new Social Security law—whose worst effects will not be felt until *after* its authors have survived the 1978 elections—is based on two premises, both false.

The first is that the number of potential contributors will continue to grow. The real but disturbing truth is that there has been a tremendous drop in the birth rate. Fewer and fewer young workers will be out there paying the bills for more and more elderly retirees.

In 1957 the national birth rate was 3.7 children per woman of childbearing age. That figure has now toppled to 1.7. The post-World War II "baby boom" is at an end. Far from facing a population explosion, which we were assured a few years back was just tick-tick-ticking away, for all intents and purposes we now face population stagnation.

There are several reasons why the birthrate will *not* reverse itself. The commercial availability of contraceptive devices is one, massive abortion-on-demand is another. The flight of housewives into the marketplace to shore up the dwindling economic prospects of the American family is yet another. The basic truth is that government *penalizes* productive parents for having children, but *rewards* the indigent for expanding their welfare offspring. Put it all together, and it means fewer and fewer workers paying more and more for those who get a government check.

The other fanciful illusion on which the new law is passed is the pipedream that inflation will drop to four percent a year and that workers' incomes will increase 1.75 times faster than the cost of living. Does *anyone* really believe this nonsense?

As a new fiscal year began in July 1978, the feds gloomily announced a 1978 inflation rate of seven percent, with a 6.5 percent projection for 1979. Both figures were considerably higher than earlier estimates. But within months both had to be raised again. The difference in a few percentage points spells the difference in whether unemployment goes up or down, how many more workers are on the dole, and gives some indication of how much more taxes from the dwindling number of employed, productive persons will be necessary to fill the gap.

"Depression babies" who entered adulthood during the 1950s are now middle-aged citizens. They are being followed in the work force by droves of "baby-boom" Americans, who are competing for jobs and positions on all rungs of the employment ladder—at a time when employment opportunities are shrinking instead of expanding.

The middle-agers find their way up the ladder blocked by a glut of senior employees who understandably want to hold on as long as they can to their salaries, before being cast into the "security" of an old age "covered" by "benefits" which are only bestowed if the breadwinner makes no more than $4,000 a year.

It is these middle-income wage earners middle-aged and younger, their employers, and the self-employed who will pay more and more for benefits they are less and less likely to receive. The effects on the economy of such a system will be disastrous.

While employees will put in bigger and bigger "contributions" every year, particularly after 1978, employers will have to match these chunks. The only conceivable outcome of this has to mean higher prices for their products and the reduction of the numbers of employees they hire, two more additional factors in inflation.

The corporate giants and conglomerates which employ many thousands of people, such as General Motors, Ma Bell and its subsidiaries, U.S. Steel, and the like, can pass on the multi-million-dollar tax increases to consumers in higher prices for automobiles, telephone service, and manufactured goods.

It's difficult to realize, today, that when the Social Security scheme was first foisted on the American people in 1937, the *total* tax paid per worker was $60 a year—$30 for the employer, $30 for the employee. Ten years later it was the same. But by 1957 it had tripled to $189; by 1967 it was $581; and 10 years later it was $1,950. This *combined* rate will be $6,092 in 1987. In 1940, when only 60 percent of the work force was involved in the program, the average monthly benefit was $36.40. The figure was $344 in 1975, in large part because of the rise in inflation. Had Social Security *not* kept pace with inflation, the 1975 average payout would have been less than $174.

Initially, Social Security was promoted as a way to provide a modest supplement to the income of retired workers in commerce and industry. But over the years, benefits were increased, coverage was expanded, new programs were added, and new dependents were brought in.

If Social Security were dropped lock, stock and barrel today, it would need well over $4 *trillion* in additional funds simply to pay its present obligations. That is more than $20,000 for every single person in the country! Social Security is not only bankrupt, it is bankrupt many times over.

As Warren Brookes, the brilliant economic journalist for the *Boston Herald American,* puts it, Social Security is:

nothing but a national economic tragedy—a huge economic disaster.... It has turned out this way because its underlying premise is fraudulent. There is no way to run a responsible social insurance pension scheme unless it is funded, and Social Security has never been funded. Put simply, there is no way to make a "chain letter" or a "pyramid" game work, even with the use of the government force of taxation.

As more and more Americans are realizing, Social Security is a massive swindle—probably the largest of all time. It can best be likened to a gigantic Ponzi scam, which took investors for millions of dollars back in the 1920s. Ponzi was a Brooklyn con man who promised investors phenomenal profits on his secret deals. For a while, the scam appeared to work, as he was able to use money from new depositors to keep the old ones happy—and spreading the good news. Eventually, however, the truth got out; no new investors could be found, the ones already taken to the cleaners got mad, and Ponzi got taken to jail.

Ponzi, you see, lacked one thing that Social Security uses to keep its scheme going: the power of government to *force* people to "contribute" to what they know is a losing proposition.

As in most Ponzi frauds, the initial investors often do quite well. The success quotient is essential to lure in more suckers. The first beneficiaries of Social Security did collect more than they paid in through taxes. But the longer a Ponzi scheme continues, the more new investors must be suckered in to support it. Finally, it collapses. Congress can bail out the Social Security hustle for a while, by continuing to raise taxes. But sooner or later, the pigeon will squawk. Or, there simply won't be anymore meaningful taxes to raise.

In the Ponzi con game, the true nature of the financial scheme is hidden so that the overall operation

seems attractive—an exact description of how Social
Security has been sold to the American people. It has
been sold as an old age and disability insurance program. In truth, it is simply another income-transfer
and welfare plan.

Just as in the Ponzi swindle, the first few sharpies
who figured out what was happening, and tried to warn
other investors, were ridiculed, scorned, and ignored.
For decades, Social Security has been as sacred to many
Americans as baseball, apple pie, and coffee breaks.

It is utterly astounding to realize that the vast majority of Americans still believe that, force or no, their
Social Security "contributions" enter a "fund" in their
name, one which is stored for them until the golden
moment of retirement, when it all becomes available as
a payback. Nothing, of course, could be further from the
truth. *All Social Security collections go into the general
fund and are spent each year*. Each and every penny
collected in the name of Social Security over the years
has long ago been spent. The government made off with
the cash and left behind an IOU in the form of a bond.

Practically nobody understands how the system really works. Nobody is *supposed* to. Back in 1965, Bar-
ron's quoted an obviously anonymous Social Security
official as admitting: "Continued general support for
the Social Security system hinges on continued public
ignorance of how the system works. I believe that we
have nothing to worry about because it is so enorm-
ously complex that nobody is going to figure it out."

The Social Security propaganda mill never bothers to
inform its "contributors" *or* its recipients that Social
Security is not secure. That it has *nothing* to do with
storing up an individual fund which will pay you off
later in life, like interest on a savings account or a
legitimate retirement plan. It is *packaged* that way,

willfully and deceitfully, but it is *not* a fund for old-age insurance. This is the biggest of the Big Lies protecting this socialist boondoggle.

Social Security is simply a federally funded Ponzi confidence game. It is one that is "transgenerational" in scope—that is, retirees are *not* being paid out of the fruits of the salaries that they themselves earned while employed earlier. Everything you and your employer are "contributing" today is being paid out now to those who are already collecting. The only way you will ever collect is to tax future generations to pay for it. But the number of potential contributors is dropping as the birth rate declines *and* more and more workers take jobs with government — which is exempt from the system.

For forty-one years the promoters of Social Security have sold it to the American people as "insurance." But it has never been an insurance program. At its very inception, it was called "federal old age benefits." Not a word about insurance occurred in the original Act of 1935.

The scheme was barely off the ground when it was challenged before the U.S. Supreme Court. Social Security lawyers knew they dare not call the snake oil they were peddling "insurance," because any effort of the government to promote compulsory insurance would indeed be unconstitutional. So the system's own lawyers argued before the high court:

> *The Act creates no contractual obligation with respect to the payment of benefits. The court has pointed out the difference between insurance which creates vested interests and pensions and other gratuities involving no contractual obligations. The Act cannot be said to constitute a plan for compul-*

sory insurance within the accepted meaning of the term "insurance."

That was the line peddled to the Supreme Court in 1937. It is in complete contrast with the propaganda spoon-fed the American public. We are supposed to believe that Social Security *is* insurance, and that somehow our share in it is guaranteed. Social Security secured a favorable ruling, one based on Social Security's own assurances that the system did *not* envision a "contractual obligation with respect to the payment of benefits."

During that 1937 challenge, the Social Security Administration also told the Court:

These [alleged "contributions"] are true taxes, their purpose being simply to raise revenue. The proceeds are paid unrestricted into the Treasury as internal revenue collections, available for the general support of the government.

In 1939, *after* admitting it is a tax, not insurance, Social Security changed its name to "Old Age and Survivors Insurance Benefits." And ever since that early date, the notion that Social Security is as American as apple pie, and is something everyone has a "right" to expect, whether there are any real benefits or not, has been bought, hook, line and sinker, by a befuddled public.

Throughout four decades of propaganda, Social Security apologists have used the phrase "trust funds" with the abandon of a mosquito at a nudist camp. They have contrived the illusion that in some vast vault somewhere there are great stacks of Social Security money accumulating to be paid out over the years to grateful recipients.

In March, 1978, *U.S. News & World Report,* doing a question-and-answer rundown on Social Security "trust funds," observed that "the government dips into that money" to spend it elsewhere, but added this is done "only as a loan. The trust funds get Treasury securities in exchange. In effect, the government borrows money by selling securities to the funds. Thus, the securities in the trust funds represent a debt of the U.S. government... ."

Yes, and there's the rub. The mounting debts of the U.S. government are somehow, some way, to be paid by future generations. But increasingly, that future is now. *Our* tax bills are going up astronomically, as the bills for previous generosity are now coming due.

The Bank for International Settlements in Switzerland puts it succinctly:

> *The U.S. government has borrowed every penny of the Social Security reserve and spent it. The workers' cash was replaced by government bonds, which are merely the government's IOU's. Like the public gold in Fort Knox, their money is gone with the wind.*

In 1979, more than half of the workers in America will find—if they check—that they are paying *more* in Social Security taxes than their bill for income taxes. Yet not a single penny of this incredible rake-off is being saved to pay them anything. No sooner is it deposited in Washington than it goes pouring back out—at the rate of more than one billion dollars a day.

The entire con is dependent on the ignorance and the apathy of the victim, as one Social Security official admitted over ten years ago. It is not "social" and it is not "secure." It is a tax—a particularly cruel and deceptive tax, because half of it is hidden in the price of goods we buy, and our politicians are not honest with us about the half we do see!

Suffice it to say that if a private company ran a retirement fund or insurance program the way Social Security is operated, its leaders would be imprisoned for fraud.

Like most parts of the federal monster now strangling the American population, there is no painless solution to the problem of Social Security. But it *is* clear that changes must be made—the quicker the better—before it takes us all to the poorhouse.

The means must be found, of course, to make sure that the existing retirees are not shortchanged. But while emergency funds continue to provide for them, there should be the most profound encouragement for young people entering the system to look elsewhere for their retirement and insurance benefits.

Perhaps Social Security of a kind can still continue, but it should never, *never* be compulsory. Taxpayers should have the same right that federal employees and legislators have regarding Social Security. In other words, you and I should be able to tell a greedy, spendthrift, dishonest bureaucracy, "Include me out!"

Chapter Eight
The Endangered Businessman

Childhood dreams of almost every adult included growing up to become successful. Through hard work and determination, we intended to become successful, independent, honored and admired. We might do it by starting a business which never before existed. Or offering a service which would revolutionize an entire field. Some of us even dreamed about changing the living patterns of all Americans.

It was a good dream, and it was passed on from generation to generation not because it always came true, but because it was *possible* that it could. Part of the promise of America to every little boy and girl was that the only real limitation to their beckoning horizon was their own ability and determination.

As with so many dreams, this one is ending, too. Today, bureaucratic guidelines often limit the scope of possible success, well before talent and even effort determine the future of a small business.

How bad has the situation become? There are now more than 7,000 different kinds of federal forms that small businesses must complete weekly, monthly, quarterly, or annually. State and local reports (many due only to federal mandate) can double or triple that number.

Every day, hundreds, sometimes thousands, of new bureaucratic rules and standards are published in the *Federal Register*. Each agency and department has but to print a new rule in the *Federal Register* and sud-

denly, without Congress doing anything, a new law is
on the books. So popular has this method of *bureaucratic* rule-making become that the *Federal Register*
now has more than double the number of pages in the
Encyclopaedia Britannica!

Even so devoted an advocate of Big Government as
Senator Gaylord Nelson agrees that the problem has
become critical. "Our small businesses are sinking
deeper into a morass of federal rules, regulation, and
paper," he says. "They are victimized by discriminatory
federal income-tax laws. They are being driven out of
business by confiscatory estate taxes."

The effect of all this? The Senator says it is no longer
a question of convenience or even displeasure. For
many Americans trying to earn their own way through
their own small business, it is now a matter of *survival!*
"We have an important new matter of concern to
America. This new issue — the health of independent
small business — involves the vital, economic, social,
sociological and philosophical questions. It involves the
question of survival of a competitive free enterprise
system."

In other words, small business is being crushed by
bureaucrats and regulators run amuck. A "small" business is usually defined as a company with fewer than
500 employees and less than one million dollars in
annual sales. Such firms comprise 97 percent of all
United States businesses; they provide 52 percent of
non-government employment, 48 percent of total business output, and half of all innovative and technological developments. Clearly, our country cannot exist
without them. But these courageous entrepreneurs are
facing elimination at the hands of a government they
have supported for more than 200 years.

C. Jackson Grayson, Jr., head of the Price Commission for Nixon's Economic Stabilization Program, minced no words in predicting elimination of the free-market system as we know it today:

> *I am not saying that there is and will continue to be public regulation of the private enterprise system. Since 1930, we have had that—a mixed public-private system. But in the 1970's, the pendulum of the mix has been swinging further, and faster, toward central control. Call it what you will—managed capitalism, socialism, a post-industrial state—the end result will be the virtual elimination of the free-market system as we know it.*

Freedom of enterprise diminishes, of course, in direct proportion to governmental regulation imposed upon it. And the power of federal bureaucrats over American business today is awesome.

The Consumer Product Safety Commission, for example, has virtually limitless authority over all products in the marketplace. "You name it and CPSC probably has jurisdiction over it,"crowed Richard Simpson, the commission's first chairman. The CPSC has the authority to ban or recall products from the market, without so much as a court hearing, simply by issuing a determination that the offensive item is unsafe. It can order rebates to consumers and even send offending executives to jail.

How capriciously can such power be used? Consider the absolute nightmare visited upon a small toy company which manufactured plastic baby rattles. In trying to meet federal regulations, it also very nearly met its death. Marlin Toy Products of Horicon, Wisconsin, nearly went bankrupt, despite consistent compliance with federal edicts. The problem began when the Food and Drug Administration decided that the plastic chips in Marlin's rattles might be dangerous to a child if the rattle broke and they were swallowed. There was no evidence this had ever happened, you understand. Government bureaucrats were merely playing their favorite game of "What if..." So the FDA put Marlin's rattles on its list of banned toys.

The company subsequently redesigned the product and removed the offending chips, then informed the newly created CPSC of its action. The Consumer Product Safety Commission got in the act because it had taken over administration of the Federal Hazardous Substances Act.

Along came the next holiday season, and a new list of hazardous toys was issued. Marlin officials couldn't believe their eyes—the rattles were still banned! When this was called to the commission's attention, the company was told that a *proof reading* error had taken place. The rattles weren't *really* banned—but it was impossible to recall the 250,000 lists just to delete the listing of one company's now-safe product!

Of course, despite the fact that the rattles were now "safe," even by CPSC standards, stores across the country cancelled orders for the product. The Marlin people lost $1.2 million in sales—and had absolutely no recourse against the government. That's the way the rattle revolves, don't you know. Forget about the officers and owners, investors and stockholders; they didn't get any sympathy in Washington where "profit" is considered a four-letter word. In addition to lost earnings, a full 75 percent of Marlin's work force (read that: human beings struggling for an honest living) had to be laid off from their jobs. And the Big Brother regulators stifle a barely polite yawn.

The litany of troubles from small firms in every part

of the country is endless. Andrew Ross, owner of two variety stores in Norwalk, Connecticut, is concerned about the bigger payments he must make for his employees' Social Security and unemployment insurance. "I laid off one employee and my unemployment compensation rate went up 6 percent for two years," he complains.

Others are anxious over the phony, federally-fueled tide of consumerism, which they believe places more demands on small companies than on bigger competitors.

One example is the skyrocketing cost of product liability insurance that firms have to bear as the result of more frequent lawsuits. Surveys by the National Federation of Independent Business indicate that many firms had never had a product liability claim against them but are paying 500 to 1000 percent more in insurance premiums than they did just a few years ago.

Charles Brewer, a small plastics manufacturer in Anaheim, California, paid $2,000 for his insurance six years ago. Last year he was unable to even obtain insurance. His former insurance company told him that perhaps Lloyd's of London would insure him—at a cost of about $40,000 a year.

The hurdles go on and on—so much that the Senate Small Business Committee estimates that a new firm stands only about a 25-percent chance of survival.

Blame for such a tragic record in what was once the strongest free-enterprise system in the world must be laid directly at the foot of recklessly burgeoning government, which debilitates American small business through suffocating paperwork requirements, ridiculous rules and impossible regulations, and, of course, taxes, taxes, taxes.

A few years ago, Congress established a Commission

on Federal paperwork, to determine just how pervasive, and perverse, are the tentacles of federal regulation that are slowly strangling business in America.
When the Commission's report was finished, Rep. G.
William Whitehurst said it proved conclusively that
federal paperwork "is slowly but effectively stifling the
free-enterprise system." The Congressman wasn't just
whistling past the file cabinets; consider the implications of the following findings by the amazed investigators:

• Government agencies print about 10 billion forms a
year to be completed by U.S. business. That is enough
to fill more than 4 *million* cubic feet of space.

• Each year the U.S. public spends about $40 billion
to complete all that paperwork. The federal government spends another $15 billion a year just to process
and file it.

• Small business spends about $18 billion completing
its share of the paperwork pyramid.

• The federal government spends another $1 billion
for directives accompanying its forms.

• Businesses with 50 employees or less complete
approximately 75 to 80 types of forms every year.

• One business, with 40,000 employees, maintains
125 file drawers of records to meet Federal reporting
requirements.

• A company operating three small TV stations filed
45 *pounds* of forms with its license-renewal application.

• A radio station in New Hampshire paid $26 *in
postage alone,* to mail its application to Washington.

• Each year the federal government issues a two-
mile stack of quarterly wage-report forms for business
to complete. Checking them, counting them, and filing

them keeps a lot of bureaucrats out of the unemployment lines!

• A typical small business with gross income under $30,000 is required to file 53 separate *tax* forms in the course of the year, not to mention scores of other reports from other agencies and bureaus.

• The State of Maryland refused a $60,000 HEW grant for a consumer education program, because the cost of completing the forms would use up approximately 75 percent of the grant!

• The Department of Agriculture maintains 989,224 cubic feet of records. That astronomical total is increasing by 64,631 cubic feet of paper every year, almost 36,500 file drawers. The Department spends $150 million yearly on forms, reports and supporting systems.

• A stack of one sample of all the various census forms measures 6 feet high.

• Official records stored around the country total 11.6 million cubic feet, an amount eleven times larger than the volume of the Washington monument.

• Costs of federal paperwork five years ago totaled more than the federal government's *combined* expenditures for health, education, welfare, saving the environment, community development, and housing.

If you think the paperwork burden on small business is breath-taking, when you get to larger corporations the cost becomes simply mind-boggling. The Commission on Federal Paperwork reports that one oil company spends $17 million a year, and keeps nearly 500 persons working full-time, just to file reports with the various federal agencies that demand them. And this does not even include their income, payroll, profit, and tax reports, which are handled in another department!

The commission cited the case of another oil company (without mentioning it by name) that files 8,800 reports annually with eighteen separate government bureaus and agencies. The total included:

- 1,095 reports to the Environmental Protection Agency, including daily reports on each of the three types of pollution—waste water discharge, outfall water discharge, and emissions of air pollution.
- 799 reports to the Coast Guard, including two daily shipping reports.
- 521 reports to the Bureau of Mines, including a daily report of "respirable dust samples."
- 342 reports to the U.S. Geological Survey, including a weekly progress report.
- 52 reports to the Federal Energy Administration on the weekly stock of oil in refineries and pipelines.

"This is merely representative of the number of reports filed by the larger corporations each year," notes C.C. Candee, a business liaison for the Paperwork Commission.

But even this awesome litany tells only part of the story. Whenever you see an article or hear a comment about the cost to business of complying with federal regulations, please keep in mind two things. First, whatever estimate you have heard can be *doubled;* no matter what business spends to comply with government, government spends at least as much establishing and maintaining the very agencies and bureaus doing the regulating! And needless to say, all of this is financed by *you,* the unhappy and beleaguered taxpayer.

Second, you also pay all of the costs to business of this mountain of paperwork and petty rule-making. Any business—from the largest car manufacturer to the smallest dry cleaner—has only one way to recover these costs: by charging more for its product or service. Big business may not be happy about the situation, but it knows you'll continue to buy cars, and furniture, and fuel. But for many small firms and stores, more government regulation means the death-knell, as once proud and independent merchants are soon in the unemployment line, or working for someone else. Either way, another source of new jobs (and more taxes) has disappeared.

It is true that, even if we had the most honest and most responsible bureaucrats in the world running the present system, we would all still be in danger. There is simply too much power, too much authority, too much *cost* involved in perpetuating this Frankenstein's monster of bureaucracy. It *must* be reduced. The *quantity* of government is simply too great today. But the *quality* we are getting leaves a lot to be desired, too.

Right now, this is being written, the newspapers are filled with accounts of multi-million dollar scandals in the General Services Administration. This is the agency responsible for buying all of the office equipment, supplies, pencils and paperclips and photocopiers used each year by the hordes of government clerks, typists, and secretaries. To no one's surprise, we are learning that the officials in charge are stealing us blind.

Last year, the Department of Health, Education, and Welfare admitted that it *lost* approximately $7 billion. That is, somehow the agency spent 7,000 million dollars in 1977—but can find no record of where the money went! That is the equivalent of all the taxes paid by all of the citizens of fifteen of our states. It is enough to purchase one million luxury automobiles. Yet it represents only *five* percent of HEW's total budget! Is it any wonder there is considerable financial hanky-panky going on behind Washington's closed doors?

Of all the absurd and onerous government agencies binding small business, perhaps greatest of all is the Occupational Safety and Health Administration. The wretched excesses of OSHA have been exposed time and time again nationally, but not all of the agency's bad deeds are easily visible. There is simply no way to measure the jobs lost or never created as a result of the time, effort, and money needed by employers to fend off the Oshacrats.

It has been estimated that the cost of business in general has been increased as much as 30 percent because of OSHA regulations alone. For years, Oshacrats have violated the Constitution with impunity, in searches without warrants. That, at last, may be changing—thanks to courageous challenges from a couple of independent businessmen. But the agency *continues* to act as prosecutor, judge, and jury. No rule is too insignificant if it can be interpreted to make life more difficult for an employer.

One business, reported Congressman Dan Quayle, "was ordered to have signs printed in both Spanish and English since there was one employee of Spanish descent. The only problem with this is the Spanish employee only speaks English."

A constituent of Arkansas Senator Dale Bumpers was fined "because the toilet paper in a portable toilet was not hung on a hanger."

Senator Wendell Ford tells about a small manufacturer who was moving his business the day an OSHA inspector came by and was fined because a ladder was leaning against the building he was vacating.

There seems to be no limit to this federal folly. The *Richmond News Leader* tells about a dam being built in

Michigan. "OSHA is requiring that construction workers at the site wear life preservers," the paper reports, "even though the river has been diverted to a new course more than five miles from the dam site."

Meanwhile, an inspection of OSHA's headquarters uncovered hundreds of violations of its own regulations. But federal agencies are not required to comply with OSHA mandates! Your bureaucratic masters are not about to practice what they preach. They have made government agencies, offices, and activities immune to their own standards for business.

In 1978, head Oshacrat Eula Bingham announced a program to "Switch to Common Sense Priorities." Then she promptly proposed a regulatory policy for "cancer-causing" substances so wild as to provoke the temperate *Business Week* to call it "mindless." So anti-business is this gang that it contends economic feasibility should not even be considered in requiring compliance with its standards.

The bad press forced OSHA to propose dropping 1,100 rules from its enforcement efforts. But first, *all* the general industry regulations which cover workers and employers will be republished in the *Federal Register*. The regulations which OSHA proposes to delete will be noted. Then the agency will ask for public comment for 90 days; public hearings will probably be scheduled to discuss the changes. Only after all this will the revised regulations go into effect.

A skeptic might predict that some of the endangered regulations will be rewritten and thus survive. But even if the total 1,100 are dropped, they amount to only 10 percent of the total rules.

And if these changes *do* occur, should not we taxpayers expect a 10 percent reduction in the agency work force and budget? Of course, no such thought has even been considered—even though just one such rule resulted in 4,027 violations being processed.

Big Brother lovers maintain that, without OSHA, greedy or callous employers will stand by and let their workers get maimed. Baloney! Good workers are hard to find these days. And no employer wants to get sued or have his insurance rates go sky high. The ridiculous demands by tyrannical Oshacrats simply add to the cost of all products we buy and therefore reduce our standard of living.

Dr. Murray Weidenbaum of the Center for the Study of American Business at Washington University, who himself was once a federal bureaucrat, says there is a multiplier effect of about twenty times. That is, whatever the total expenditures of government to support its regulatory activities, twenty times that amount must be spent in the private sector to comply with the regulations. Professor Weidenbaum estimates that the total cost of federal regulation, alone, in Fiscal 1979 could easily rise to one hundred billion dollars—about seven percent of the projected Gross National Product. Does anybody really believe we are getting a hundred billion dollars' worth of health, safety, or protection for our money?

Yet even this does not begin to measure the true cost of regulation. Most people don't think of what does *not* get produced because of government policies. The jobs that are *not* created. The taxes that are *not* paid. The services that are *not* available to you and me. A study by the Brookings Institution on the effects of regulations concludes that federal regulation is holding back expansion by as much as twenty-five percent. Industry is spending billions to comply with insane government regulations that produce no additional cars, or washing machines, or tons of steel.

Through most of the post-war years until the late 1960s, real U.S. annual production growth increased by at least 2.5 percent per year. More recently, the growth rate has been at about two percent, and in recent months it has been zero. During this same period of time, government spending has shot up faster than a rocket taking off for the moon. Where will it end? A peek into any socialized country reveals the answer.

For a moment, let's forget about ideology, let's forget politics, let's even forget the black-booted terror of a police state. Focus with me on this one unique difference between the United States and almost every other country around the world: We have tens of thousands of salesmen, whose job is to *persuade* us to purchase their goods. In every socialist country, the job of salesman is unknown. Instead, they have millions of ration clerks, whose job is to divide up the "too little"—to decide who will be *allowed* to have how much.

For two hundred years, this country has been the "land of opportunity" for millions of our citizens. We were able to work and to sweat, to plan and to produce, and—most important of all—we were free to keep the fruits of our own labors. Because of this freedom, our forefathers created an economic miracle. With only six percent of the world's population, and about seven percent of the world's natural resources, they created almost fifty percent of the world's goods! They created "too much." We shared much of it with the rest of the world, becoming the most charitable people that ever existed. While in this country, salesmen competed to give us better prices, better products, better services. We achieved so much prosperity that even our poorest lived better than all but the *rulers* of most other nations.

Now, that dream may be ending. To our children and

our children's children, it may become a faint memory. As Abraham Lincoln observed over a century ago, "If destruction be our lot, we ourselves will be its authors and executioners." It is not too late to restore this dream—but it *is* too late to procrastinate any longer!

Chapter Nine
As The Lights Go Out

There was a time, not so long ago, when the American standard of living, the bottom-line proof and payoff of the free enterprise system, was the most coveted way of existence on the planet.

We held our heads high throughout the world—even when curbside Marxists baited us with "Yankee, go home!" (While in *sotto voce* suggesting, "but leave the cash behind.") We *knew*—as Harry Truman used to say—that "we never had it so good." Lines of immigrants from war-ravaged Europe and Asia joined those from Latin America to enter the land where dreams come true.

No one can yet deny that Americans are among the most "affluent" people on earth, if by affluence we means more access to more gadgets and more food than anyone else.

But the dollar no longer reigns supreme. It is being embarrassingly traded off by foreign tourists as fast as they can cram Japanese yen, Swiss francs, and West German deutschmarks into their suitcases. Americans stranded in Europe during the dollar batterings of the mid-1970s well remember the sudden 20 percent hikes in their hotel bills and were staggered to learn many foreign shops were not even *accepting* those little green passports to bliss which once proudly stood "as good as gold."

Well, despite the dollar battering, don't we still have the highest salary and educational levels on earth? No.

In terms of per capita earning power, the U.S.A. has already slipped behind part of Scandinavia. In terms of literacy and basic education we are trailing Switzerland and Japan. And the quality of education in this country has plummeted geometrically in three decades.

With young couples hardly able to buy a home, and with both of them forced to work to make ends meet, with both breadwinners and their offspring facing mugging and mayhem down the street or in school, the United States has suddenly become a place to which the more affluent of several European countries no longer have a hankering to immigrate.

Three years ago, embarrassingly enough, the French Navy circulated maps of New York City to its shore-leave-bound mariners. The maps were divided into two sections: "Dangerous by Night" and "Dangerous by Night *and* Day."

Let's face it: America's standard of living, America's bright promise for her citizens, America herself, simply aren't what they used to be.

We detail elsewhere how the regulations which are churned out from our polyfaceted governmental bureaucracy annually to fold, bend, staple and mutilate citizens—a total of $140 billion per year in costs alone—are hamstringing, hampering, tying down, prying into, thwarting and undercutting "the good life."

As giant government has crept more and more into American life, under the guise of providing "freedom from want"—a freedom never contemplated by the framers of the U.S. Constitution—the liberty to succeed has diminished to the point that a quarter of all Americans provides 70 percent of Big Government's tax base. While this goes on, American workers are failing to keep pace with wages for comparable jobs in other countries, and government rules, edicts, and regulations stifle almost every aspect of day-to-day existence.

The productive American today is not only tax-strapped as he ekes out a financial existence (and supports two other bureaucrats and one welfare recipient through the fruit of his toil), he is also told by environmentalists that everything he does has polluted the environment. While made to feel guilty over working for and owning an automobile, he must literally be strapped into it lest warning bells sound, and he starts salivating like one of Professor Pavlov's penned puppies.

Should he dare to open a small business, he finds himself awash in a sea of local, state, and federal red-tape, which can ruin him should a rusty nail be found behind the cupboard or the employee he has just hired not turn out to be the statutorily mandated female Hottentot of doubtful sexual preference.

It is all for "his own good" and the good of society, of course, because central planning—always backed, ultimately, by central *coercion*—looks to the safety and security of the collective whole. This means regulations for housing, food, schools, clothing, health, automobiles, and all other aspects of technological, industrialized society. The total control over our lives that we are seeing is excused as part of the natural flow of history; the acceptance of planning, regulation, and coercion is understood as necessary to our very survival. Hogwash!

The more the regulators get into the safety business, the more unsafe things become. Remember one of the last hurrahs of the Ford Administration, when the President himself went before national television to alert Americans to the potential danger of swine flu? Everyone was encouraged to fall into line for federally supported swine flu shots. Only after old folks by the score had dropped dead within hours of their inoculations was this idiotic scheme quietly phased out.

Efforts to regulate highway safety have led to *more* accidents, not fewer. For instance, in 1974 the National Highway Traffic Safety Administration issued a safety standard requiring a complex antilock braking system in all commercial vehicles that use air brakes. The aim, allegedly, was to make it possible for bus and truck drivers to stop in a shorter distance without losing control of their vehicles.

How has the system turned out? Often, it has given the wrong signal, resulting in either no brakes at all, or a sudden locking—the very risk it was supposed to eliminate. It is locked brakes which cause the truck and trailer of large highway transports to jackknife.

According to one trucking company, vehicles with electronic air brakes have had four times as many jackknife accidents as those without. One West Coast trucking fleet disconnected the system in each of its new newly purchased trucks because it was so dangerous. Uncle Fed's meddling in "highway safety" proved so disastrous in this instance that the regulation, mercifully, was rescinded six months after being put into effect. The cost of its implementation, of course, was never recovered.

Salaries paid to American workers failed to keep pace with wages for comparable jobs in other countries in the first half of the 1970s, according to a Conference Board study. The report on salaries paid to beginning engineers in twelve countries suggests that the devaluation of the dollar and more rapid inflation abroad in the early 1970s were major factors in the comparative decline in American salaries for new engineers. Engineer salaries were studied because the position often serves as a benchmark for other salary levels, the Conference Board said.

When salaries were compared in dollar amounts, the U.S. engineer fell from the top spot in 1971 to fifth place 1975. Based on the number of hours of work needed to purchase 115 widely used consumer goods and services, Denmark came out on top. In 1975, engineers there had to work just 877 hours to purchase the goods that American engineers worked 1,234 hours to buy.

The two items comprising the most personal elements of the American standard of living, the ones in which those workers invest most of their earnings, are, of course, the home and the family automobile. As we detail elsewhere, governmental regulation, taxation, and inflation have combined to make buying and keeping a new home nearly impossible for millions of families.

Yet, as that one-fourth of American taxpayers struggles to meet the bureaucrats' demand for nearly three-fourths of the country's tax revenues, more and more non-productive citizens find Uncle Sugar encouraging them to let those taxpayers pick up their rent.

Four hundred thousand American families are already on the dole for rent subsidies, and up to twenty-seven million families could qualify under current guidelines from the Department of Housing and Urban Development.

Ford's HUD Secretary, Carla Hills, announced that HUD would provide rent subsidies for any family whose income is less than 80 percent of the median income of other families in the area. Apparently the government's latest poverty standard is your next-door neighbor! If you live in Washington, D.C., and make under $14,840, you qualify for federal rent subsidies.

Apartment dwellers are not the only Americans touched by HUD. Its efforts toward "urban renewal" have truly been substantial...substantially disastrous, that is.

Outspoken Senator Jesse Helms has a particularly intense disdain for HUD. In a government filled with countless potential targets for conservative wrath, HUD tops the list, according to Helms. "The federal housing program will surely go down in history as the ultimate government absurdity," he has predicted. "Presumably, the major objective of a housing program is to build houses—yet the federal housing program has given us fewer houses," Helms notes. In fact, HUD has destroyed 2½ times more dwellings than it has built! You, the taxpayer, finance both ends of this incredible see-saw, of course.

The housing program, as administered by HUD, is a notably wasteful failure, as indicated by figures supplied to a Helms aide by the Library of Congress. Those figures show that HUD tore down 538,044 houses and apartments and built only 200,687 in the period from 1967 to 1971. In case you're bristling for a more up-to-date accounting of HUD's productivity, you're in good company. Reliable figures covering demolitions in more recent years are not available because HUD claims it is no longer keeping a record. "Apparently they're tearing down so many units they can't keep track," Helms deduced wryly.

Not only is the American Dream of owning—and hanging on to—your own home under attack, but so is the ability of most Americans to own and drive an automobile.

Columnist Patrick Buchanan has given considerable thought to the all-fronts bureaucratic assault on the auto:

Of all the inventions that have liberated the working man from the drudgery of daily existence, none has done more than the automobile. It has taken him off crowded and dirty commuter buses, subways and streetcars, where he sometimes spent 90 minutes a day.

Yet, for 10 years, a political war has been mounted against the automobile. Private cars are regularly disparaged by the trendies in the media as inefficient wasters of raw materials.

They are blamed for urban sprawl, congestion, pollution and the energy crisis. Pressured by Ralph Nader and like-minded "friends of the consumer," the Congress has mandated costly styling changes, safety features and emission standards. And the consumer has paid the price.

Why this incredible antagonism toward the one invention most responsible for our freedom of mobility? Perhaps because the American car encourages such individualism, Buchanan suggests:

The motives of the anti-auto crowd are varied. There is first the snobbish disparagement by the elite for the mode of transportation favored by the masses. Secondly, as a statist, the modern liberal looks to government as the instrument of national deliverance.

Ideologically, he is vastly more comfortable with a government-managed, government-run transit system than with a system of hundreds of thousands of individuals in hundreds of thousands of privately owned cars.

Then, there are the economic stakes involved. The big-city media, the giant banks, the urban politi-

cians all have a vested interest in stopping the na-
tional stampede to the suburbs. And since it is the
auto which makes out-migration possible, the auto
is declared enemy.

But the American middle and working classes
have stakes here as well. In a free choice, they have
voted decisively against mass transit, and in favor
of the automobile. Today, 80 percent of the labor
force rides to work by car and 94 percent of the
inter-city trips are by auto.

But the actual cost of operating those private vehicles continues to be pushed beyond the means of many
Americans. For example, by 1977 the price of owning
and operating a new car had become 30.1 cents per mile
for the average owner, reports the Hertz Corporation's
Car Leasing Division.

This represents a seven percent increase over the
previous year. In 1976, the cost was 28.1 cents a mile,
while in 1973, it was only 20.2 cents. In the four years
from 1973 to 1977, the cost per mile rose more than in
all the 23 years from 1950 to 1972! (For you nostalgia
buffs, the average per-mile costs back in the "good old
days" of 1953 were 10.9 cents.)

This suffocating rise in the cost of automobile use
pales when compared to the potential for fiscal disaster
posed by the latest bureaucratic Frankenstein, the new
Department of Energy.

The sheer bulk of cash allotted to keep this horde of
hoarders in business would be scandalous in more sensible times. In 1978, the budget for the Department of
Energy amounted to $10,600,000,000. This budget ex-
ceeds the *total* amount of money spent in 1975 by all the
oil and natural gas producers combined in the United
States for drilling and exploration.

As well as having acquired energy functions from four cabinet departments, the Department of Energy had on its payroll during 1978 some 19,767 employees—which, when compared to its budget, represents expenditures of $500,000 per department employee.

The well-contrived background which made possible the birth of such a monstrous governmental off-spring is worthy of scrutiny. Long lines of frustrated motorists at gas stations across the country are an irritatingly fresh memory, even though it was 1973 when this side show made its debut. If Uncle Fed operated rationally, by now we should be less dependent upon the foreign supply of oil whose cutoff caused those waiting lines. Right? Wrong.

In 1960, 20 percent of our oil came from abroad. Five years ago it was 29 percent. Today the figure is approaching 50 percent. And by 1980, more than half our petroleum will be supplied by foreign sources.

Every day, rain or shine, eight million barrels of foreign oil are consumed by the American economy. In the last five years, OPEC's share of the American market has nearly doubled, from 18 to 34 percent. In other words, we are almost twice as dependent on Arab oil as we were before the embargo—and therefore twice as vulnerable. The simplest notion of market economics would encourage a supplier to raise prices under such circumstances. Water may run downhill, but oil flows where the money is.

Far from establishing our independence from foreign sources, we have been sliding ever more into their grasp. Project Independence, supposed to make us independent of the need for foreign fuel by 1980, has not even qualified as a no-win war. Virtually no shots have ever been fired!

The price we pay for this inaction could be enormous. Former Federal Energy Administrator Frank Zarb predicts that, under current conditions, another embargo would make the 1973-74 situation "look like a picnic." Former Commerce Secretary Elliott Richardson has described the possible consequences as "catastrophic."

A recent Commerce Department forecast for an extreme situation is that, if the United States lost only half its present oil imports for a year, without replacing it with Alaskan and offshore oil, "the economic toll in closed factories and businesses, in unemployment, could run as high as $170 billion in gross national product and 4.8 million jobs."

What nobody now disputes is that we have put our heads in a noose by allowing ourselves to become dependent on foreign oil for a large segment of our energy. Oil now supplies about forty-six percent of all energy consumed in the United States. That compares with twenty-nine percent for natural gas, nineteen percent for coal, four percent for hydro and other miscellaneous sources, and two percent for nuclear fuel. Without oil we face economic strangulation. It's that simple.

And what of the inevitable price hikes in petroleum we can expect from OPEC? According to energy czar Zarb, a 10 percent price hike could "cost this nation 300,000 jobs and a one percent jump in the inflation rate." A 10 percent jump in the cost of crude would add a penny per gallon to the pump price of gasoline, and cost the country nearly $4 billion.

This will be reflected in the price of everything from higher air fares to rising utility bills. Even the cost of groceries will rise as most commercial fertilizers, pesticides, insecticides, and herbicides are oil and gas derivatives.

Only when the oil has been pumped and shipped can our massive food production begin. And it is the $25 billion we get for our farm exports that allow us to buy from the OPEC cartel without wrecking ourselves on the rocks of a massive payments imbalance.

Some of our "financial experts" think our economy can absorb a 10 to 15 percent price hike with minimal damage. Possibly, even probably; but don't bet on it. The economy is unstable and the Carternomics won't help. If the 1973 boycott did not produce the recession that followed, it certainly exacerbated it. And, whether we suffer another Energy Depression in the United States, a price hike could trigger one in other nations.

Economic columnist Anthony Harrigan writes: "For many small countries, another oil price hike will be disastrous. They are likely to default on debts to lenders in the Western world. This, in turn, will cause heavy damage to Western financial institutions."

Billions of dollars in loans have been made to underdeveloped nations by major U.S. commercial banks. If these loans go into default, you can bet your last silver dime that the New York banks are not going to swallow the bad debts. The World Bank, created and controlled by these same Gotham institutions, will come riding to the rescue like the U.S. Cavalry in an old Western. The cash in its saddlebags will come from the ever-reliable U.S. taxpayers.

There is no doubt that OPEC is flexing its growing muscles more and more. The first show of strength by OPEC was in February 1971, when it announced that unless the world accepted a significant increase in oil prices it would cut off supplies. With the tacit approval of the importing countries, the big multinationals acquiesced to this demand.

The pacts they signed with the OPEC nations sent oil

prices, and consequently the "take" of the governments, rocketing at a rate unprecedented in the history of the international oil industry. Arab oil sold for 88 cents a barrel in 1968; $1.50 in 1972; just before the Arab embargo of 1973, the price was $2.32 per barrel. In 1978, the price had approached $15 per barrel!

What drives the economically ignorant berserk is that it costs only about 15 cents to pump a barrel of crude out of the ground. The unsophisticated among us can't understand why the sheiks won't be good fellows and sell their oil at 50 cents per barrel, keeping a hefty 70 percent profit for themselves. Sad to say, the oil barons make the Boston Strangler look like a saint.

But a closer look at the multinational oil companies is necessary to understand America's self-defeating role in the energy crisis.

First, it should be remembered that there are thousands of corporations involved in the petroleum industry, but the world-wide oil business is dominated by what is known as "The Seven Sisters"—Exxon, Texaco, Mobil, Standard of California, Gulf, Shell, and British Petroleum.

A review of the history of Standard Oil (now, of course, Exxon) shows that in many of its dealings it has hardly been a model to which proponents of free enterprise could point with pride. This is because the Rockefeller family, which created Standard Oil, has never been a supporter of free and open competition; their game-plan has always been a corporate monopoly.

Although at one time Standard did control 90 percent of the refining capacity in this country, the world oil business has simply been too big for any one corporation to monopolize. Thus Standard has had to settle for a cartel, with itself first among equals.

Standard's methods will never be found in an Ayn

Rand novel glorifying the self-reliant, creative, productive, politician-despising businessman who welcomes any and all challengers in the marketplace. It has specialized in political intrigue, bribery, corruption, and conspiracy.

Ever willing to go along in order to get along, the Seven Sisters have settled for an affair of convenience with OPEC. Even though OPEC countries have nationalized their oil fields, they did not send the great multinationals packing. The giants still operate the fields, drill new wells, refine the oil, transport the crude, and market the finished products.

Nationalization, in appearance or in fact, has not cut the profits of "the majors." They are bigger than ever. With the price at close to $15 per barrel instead of 88 cents, there is a much bigger pie to divide. Plus, there is the added advantage that the more effective cartel in oil has virtually knocked the independents out of the international oil business. The Seven Sisters were not sorry to see their little brothers frozen into limbo. The independent oil firms have had no leverage over nationalizing nations, since they haven't had the political influence over our own government that the Seven Sisters have.

The U. S. State Department, often last to defend America's (and Americans') interests around the world, has tacitly encouraged Third World nations to nationalize (that is, *steal*) the property of certain American corporations. So the American independent may risk five hundred million dollars to prove out a new oil field, and if the company is successful it will be denounced as a vicious exploiter and the development will be seized.

Of course, if the field proves unsuccessful that is just tough—kiss your $500 million goodbye. Which is why all but the politically-wired giants are becoming very leery about foreign oil development. The only winners in this situation have been OPEC and the Seven Sisters. The losers are the independent oil firms...and the American consumers.

The obvious lesson from all this is that the United States must make every effort to become increasingly independent of foreign fuel sources. This does not necessarily mean that we must be totally independent — that would probably be too costly. But we should encourage sufficient development to remain relatively independent while requiring the U.S. Government to use its leverage on the side of the American people, instead of being a lackey for the Seven Sisters and encouraging tin-horn dictators to wipe out independent developers.

Unfortunately, as we have noted, just when the U.S. desperately needs more petroleum production our output is sinking. "Liberals" are perennially complaining that America's energy crisis stems from the fact that we have never had an energy policy. The truth is that we have had lots of policies—and they have all helped the giant oil producers at the expense of everyone else. While it would take a separate book on the subject to chronicle all of the energy-subversive policies of the federal government, the two that stand out as having contributed most to our current energy problems are the fifteen-year quota system on foreign crude and the nation's tax laws on foreign petroleum development.

Despite the fact that the quota system was in force and supposed to stimulate domestic production, the foreign tax credit sent capital development funds to places like Mauritania, Mozambique, Papua, Equatorial Guinea, the Gulf of Thermaic, the East China Sea, and the Gulf of Thailand.

Not only were wells drilled in these faraway places with those strange sounding names, but *refineries* were also built overseas. From the mid-1960s until 1973, fewer than a half-dozen new refineries with capacities exceeding fifty thousand barrels a day were constructed here. At the same time, dozens were built abroad by Americans.

By the time the oil companies were ready to resume building domestic refineries, the Rockefeller-financed ecology boys had taken over and made it all but impossible for any but the giants to cut through the red tape and obtain the necessary permits. At the same time, the big oil companies have been able to lay the entire blame at the feet of the bug chasers.

So, when the Arab oil embargo came along, the United States was dependent on foreign oil and short of refining capacity.

The problem is not that we lack plentiful energy resources, but that the government now makes it all but impossible properly to develop them. Consider the state of our oil reserves.

There is considerable disagreement among geologists as to how much oil may be ultimately recoverable from U.S. soil, but the figure of one hundred billion barrels is, at best, conservative. Most studies place it at several hundred billion barrels, excluding shale oil.

Thomas B. Medders, Jr., president of the Independent Petroleum Association of America, told a Senate Committee in 1972:

> *The (Geological) Survey now estimates 450 billion barrels of oil and 2,100 trillion cubic feet of natural gas to be recoverable by discovery of the potential resource base.*

*These recoverable sources are in the order of 100
years' supply at present rates of U.S. consumption
of both oil and gas.*

A Senate Interior Committee Report in 1972, after
reviewing many projections, said estimates of recoverable oil ranged from 575 billion to 2,400 billion barrels
of oil. Historically, the amount of recoverable oil has
always been underestimated and there is no reason to
believe that these figures are anything but conservative.

Petroleum, of course, is not our only source of energy
fuel. If there is one source that America is particularly
blessed with, it is coal. According to various estimates,
we have from 400 to 600 years' supply based on the
present rate of consumption.

"We've got coal coming out of our ears," boasts Dr.
Thomas Falkie, who heads the U.S. Bureau of Mines.
America holds 437 billion tons of known reserves. This
is equivalent to 1.8 trillion barrels of oil. It is enough
energy, according to *Forbes* magazine, to keep one
hundred million large electric generating plants going
for the next 800 years or so.

It's ten times as much energy as is contained in Saudi
Arabia's oil and 2.6 times as much as is available from
the entire world's known oil supply. And, coal can be
turned into oil and natural gas.

In addition to oil, natural gas, and coal, we have the
potential of nuclear energy. Other exotic forms of
energy, now in various stages of development, may
someday play a significant role in meeting our energy
needs.

Fine. But if we have all this potential energy, what is
the problem? Why must we kowtow to the camel king-
doms? The simple answer is that you cannot heat your

home, light your office, or run your car on *potential* energy. We need the real thing—and I don't mean a Coca-Cola. This country cannot run on oil, natural gas, or coal that is still in the ground. But government holds the reins on development. And our all-knowing bureaucrats in Washington continue to holler "Whoa!"

Congressman John Ashbrook has summarized in the *Congressional Record* the ways in which the federal government has caused our energy shortage:

1. Banned off-shore drilling.

2. Restricted domestic drilling, especially on federal land.

3. Limited the number of refineries and the amount of oil they can refine.

4. Instituted import quotas on oil limiting the amount of foreign oil.

5. Blocked and delayed until recently the development and transportation of Alaskan oil.

6. Outlawed the use of most coal and some fuel oils because their sulfur content is "too high."

7. Forced mandatory pollution control devices on new cars that use an additional 5 billion gallons of gas a year.

8. Forced bussing of 300,000 children each day in the United States, wasting millions of gallons of gasoline yearly.

9. Delayed the development of new sources of fuel. A good example being the delay of nuclear power plants by the Federal Government and Mr. Nader.

10. Instituted Price Controls: The effect of price controls on fuel has been to increase demand and limit supply by keeping the price low.

One would think with the energy crisis becoming so obvious that red tape caused by the government bureaucrats would be cut away. But just the opposite has occurred! The United States now has more czars than Imperial Russia had in a century. Except ours are energy czars, men who seem dedicated to the concept that you can't fuel all the people all the time. "The public be dimmed" is their motto. Will an oil field displace a kangaroo rat? Don't drill. Will the salamander be jeopardized if we construct a refinery? Cancel the plans. Will the pupfish be endangered by off-shore drilling? Heaven forbid!   Even back in August of 1973, columnist Ralph de Toledano saw what was happening and warned:

> *When you get right down to it, the environmentalists are pushing for a no-growth rate in the economy, a kind of anti-expansionist paralysis. No growth for our energy industries means no growth for coming generations—because without an expanding energy production there can be no new industries, no new jobs, in these United States. This can only mean a significant drop in the standard of living.*

Yet another policy which deprives us of oil is that by which the government controls the prices.

Keeping petroleum prices artificially low is politically popular, to be sure. After all, everybody would like to have a gallon of gasoline for 30 cents. We'd like hamburger at 25 cents a pound, too. But inflation has at least doubled the prices of everything we use and gasoline is no exception. To inflation we must add the scarcity factor. The easily obtainable petroleum supplies in this country have already gone out the gas pipe.

Available petroleum now is in those places that are harder to reach. New energy sources are expensive to develop. Great risks are involved. So, as long as energy prices are kept artificially low, we are going to face shortages.

Catch 22 continues in the alternative field of coal development. Under Project Independence, America was going to double its production of coal by 1985. But according to *Forbes* of December 15, 1975: "At the rate things are going, we will be doing well to maintain today's production over the next decade."

While the Federal Government has mandated that many power companies switch from fuel oil to coal, the coal for these power companies is not being produced thanks to the Environmental Protection Agency. Again, according to *Forbes:*

> *It takes three to five years to open a surface mine and five to seven years to build an underground one. Actual construction is lagging. To date, very few of the mines that have been planned or announced are actually under construction, and most of those will be producing metallurgical coal for making steel—for which there is a robust international market—rather than steam coal for energy.*
>
> *Productivity in existing mines has been declining steadily since 1969, and no one has yet come up with a way to reverse that trend. What's the problem? Why isn't coal being developed faster? There are many problems, but the most immediate is, in a word, environmentalism ...*

For every ton of coal that could be mined but is left in the ground because of environmental radicalism, the United States will have to buy approximately 4.1 barrels of OPEC oil. At a rough estimate, mines in the eastern United States could produce 280 *million* tons a year more coal than they are currently producing. This is the equivalent of 1.1 billion barrels of oil—twelve billion dollars' worth a year. Money aside, this artificially created dependence on OPEC gives foreign governments the power to make America shiver in the cold and to close large segments of U.S. industry.

But, the Environmental Protection Agency finds Eastern coal too "dirty" to be used, and the cleaner Western coal cannot be obtained because it must be strip mined. EPA says *that* interferes with scenic wonders.

What should be done about this? One federal regulator had the gall to suggest that we'd better all just learn to take it—and we'd be a lot happier about it if we would all learn to take it with a smile! An article in the *Santa Ana Register* of November 11, 1976, headlined "Don't Resist Controls, EPA Official Tells Businessmen," gives this bureaucrat's version:

> *American businessmen can't beat those seeking to limit growth to protect the environment, so they should join them, a top federal environmental official said here Wednesday. "The time has come," said John R. Quarles, deputy administrator of the Environmental Protection Agency (EPA), "for American business leadership to stop opposing and start proposing" solutions to pollution-related problems.*
>
> *Quarles, addressing the fifth International Pollution Engineering Exposition and Congress, called for an end to what he termed "fundamentalist, knee-jerk resistance against any form of government control."*

In short: The reason we are being made miserable while being choked to death by Big Government is that we refuse to relax and enjoy it!

A far different—and far more ominous—premise is advanced by Professor P.C. Roberts. In an article entitled "Bureaucratic Conspiracy and the Energy Crisis" in *Reason* magazine, he warns:

> *We should note that the bureaucracy's perfor-mance seems incompetent only if we assume that it is striving to act in the public interest. Once we assume it is acting in its own interest, its actions appear rational.*
>
> *... Bureaucratic nests are so heavily feathered by an energy famine that the bureaucracy has a great incentive to cause one.*

The problem is that the contrived energy crisis is a time-bomb ticking away inside America. It may be a bigger threat than a nuclear explosion. The energy crisis will be used as the major excuse for wrapping this country in more and more regulations, justifying wage and price controls and rationing, and systematically destroying our economy.

There is, however, a simple and logical solution for all this nonsense. Unfortunately, it is so simple and so logical that a population long conditioned by "Liberal" polemics reels from it in horror. If we really want to solve the energy crisis we can do two things about it.

The first is to abolish the Department of Energy— and all other federal, state, and local bureaus and agencies which now block the development of vital energy.

The second is to pass a law exempting all energy producers from taxes, or at least greatly lowering the rates they must pay. The stampede of brains, energy, and capital would be so overwhelming that Americans would soon have their choice between a wide variety of competing forms of energy! Sure, some would enjoy large profits—for a while. But cutthroat competition and price cutting would follow. And instead of paying $10 billion a year for a needless, useless, *dangerous* bureaucracy, we'd see prices at the pump *and* our taxes drop. While tens of thousands of bureaucrats would have to get honest jobs, for a change. Is this really too high a price to pay?

"Liberals," of course, would wail that this amounts to turning back the clock to the dreaded Nineteenth Century—that dark epoch when this country was raised in liberty from a backward frontier to the powerhouse of this planet. But by combining the moral economic principles of the Nineteenth Century with the technology of the Twentieth we could live in the next century in both freedom and prosperity.

The choice may be as simple as this: accept the bureaucrats' premise that the only solution to a scarcity is government rationing, and watch our economy (and our freedom) be strangled. Or, encourage competition, reward endeavor, abolish the regulators, and watch supplies jump and prices drop.

It's time to say, "Enough!" It's time to call a halt, before we all start shivering to death in the dark, waiting for our ration coupons to arrive.

Chapter Ten
Fence In The Hogs!

By now, we trust we have established the point that the greatest threat to your comfort, prosperity, and financial security is the insane spendathon in Washington, D.C. To the old adage that nothing is certain in life except death and taxes, a new one can be added: If the taxocrats continue unchecked, we will all soon be *taxed to death!*

As surely as the cock will crow at sunrise, however, we can expect every politician to promise tax relief—when he is running for office. There has never been a Senator, Representative, or President elected to office on a platform of raising taxes! No, the overwhelming majority make "economy," "efficiency," "tax cuts," "spending limits," and the like a regular part of every campaign speech. It is as expected as kissing babies or eating pizza—and just about as sincere.

Since the American public has learned to trust politicians' promises about as much as they do some carnival pitchman inviting you into the sideshow, we have prepared a list of *Do's* and *Don'ts* to use in evaluating promises against performance. In deciding to launch your own "tax revolt," please remember:

Don't expect the bloated bureaucracy to reform itself. Washington has become a politician's paradise, with virtually unlimited funds to spend, countless favors to grant (and be granted), with cake and cookies galore for everyone who learns to go along with the system.

There are many federal employees who would like to see the whole mess improved. They *want* to see "civil servants" (who increasingly are seldom civil and serve only themselves) put in a honest day's work for an effective, efficient agency. The workers who will speak out, forcefully and fearlessly, to accomplish such reform, are an almost invisible minority, however. As we have already shown, most government employees learn very quickly that almost the only way to get kicked off the federal gravy train is to do or say anything about lazy, sloppy, or dishonest bureaucrats.

Don't count on the present office-holders in Congress to clean up the mess, either. By and large, they are the very ones who created it! There are a few dozen members of the House of Representatives who consistently vote against the billion-dollar boondoggles, who make a sincere effort to eliminate or greatly reduce the most damaging and irresponsible federal agencies, who refuse to "go along to get along." And perhaps half-a-dozen or so similar stalwarts in the Senate. I don't have to list their names here. Check any major newspaper or leading national magazine; they will be the ones who are constantly criticized for being "moss-backed" reactionaries, against all "progressive and humanitarian efforts." The Congressmen with the worst press are usually the *only* ones trying to stop Big Brother government from sending us all to the poorhouse.

Most "representatives of the people" are far more frightened of offending the special-interest groups, the big lobbies for increased subsidies, the governmental "experts" testifying for bigger bureaus and larger budgets, than they are worried about the voters back home catching on to the game they play. Remember, each year Congress votes on over two thousand bills. About five hundred of these will be passed. About twenty percent of those approved represent appropriations (of your tax dollars and mine) of over $1 billion a year. Many times a single bill will contain approval for twenty, fifty, or one hundred billion dollars a year—with "escalator" clauses built in that take the total further into the stratosphere in the future. Yet how often do *you* know how your Congressman votes on just *one* of these billion-dollar-plus pieces of legislation? And when your Senator or Representative does vote for legislation that adds another ten billion or so to the national debt, how often will he boast about what he's done in the next newsletter to the folks back home? Which brings me to a third *don't:*

Don't expect one hour of effort on your part, once every two or four years, to make any significant change in the way the system works. If you feel that going to the polls on the first Tuesday of November, every other year, is the only investment you need to make in trimming the size, power, and cost of government, then get ready to have everything you own, or ever hope to earn, taken from you.

But enough of the *don'ts.* It's time to get positive and discuss some of the *do's* that will produce positive change. Here are some of the things that angry and alarmed taxpayers have already shown will work, in bringing run-away government to heel.

Do make up your mind to work for a reduction in taxes—and a corresponding reduction in the size of government!—for as long as it takes to win. Howard Jarvis campaigned for Proposition 13 for fifteen years in California. After fourteen years and six months of effort, he was a failure. Six months later, he was a hero to the entire nation! There will be many battles be-

tween now and the reestablishment of fiscal sanity in
Washington. There will probably be a few losses along
the way—and even some "sunshine soldiers" who drop
out when the first tough hill looms on the horizon.

Do realize now that your first task is to get others to
share your concern … and your hope. Whether they are
willing to admit it or not, every person you know is
already involved in the battle against Big Government.
Most of them are victims. Unfortunately, while every
taxpayer is concerned about what is happening to
taxes, the declining value of the dollar, the growing bite
of inflation, the rising danger from bureaucratic des-
potism, *etc.,* far too many have allowed themselves to
become convinced that there is nothing they can do
about it.

Part of this feeling of hopelessness is deliberately
promoted by the advocates of Big Government, of
course. The parlor socialists, political prostitutes, and
bureaucratic parasites want you to believe that the
system is so massive, the pressure to maintain it so
great, the need for it so important, that any effort to
reduce the federal monstrosity is doomed to failure.

As part of this psychological assault on Americans,
the welfreeloaders make sure that every battle we lose,
every defeat we suffer, every bill that is passed over our
objections, receives more publicity than Burt Reynolds
posing nude. While every victory for fiscal sanity
somehow gets overlooked on the networks' TV news
and rates only a tiny inch or two in the back of most
newspapers. The only exception to this pattern was the
reaction to over four million Californians having the
unmitigated gall to pass Proposition 13, after every
public official in the state warned them that they would
usher in new Dark Ages if they dared try to protect
their homes and property.

Do remember that you are not alone. That millions of other Americans feel as you do. In fact, *most* citizens of this country agree that taxes are too high, government too big, spending too wasteful, politicians too dishonest, officials too irresponsible. What would happen if just a large minority of these Americans began working in concert for the same principles and programs? The thought of that happening nationally, as it did in one state, makes many bureaucrats break out in a cold sweat!

Do concentrate your efforts on the one assembly most responsible for our problems, most responsive to the public, and most effective at forcing a change. That is, the House of Representatives. *Every single spending bill must, by law, originate in the House.* Every single agency of government must, by law, submit a proposed budget to the House of Representatives every year. If your Congressman tells you there is nothing he can do to hold down spending by this agency, or reduce the power of that bureau, don't believe him.

It is not true that any agency funded by a previous Congress must be continued. It only seems that way. The House of Representatives could reduce, restrict, or eliminate every free-spending department and agency overnight, if it wanted to.

It is not true that Congress must appropriate funds for any project favored by the President. Even the Democratically-controlled majority of 1977-78 told President Carter "no" several times. Moreover, Congress can also force a reduction despite a President's objection; a two-thirds majority can even override a Presidential veto.

It is not true that Congress must appropriate funds for whatever projects the courts say are necessary, from the current madness of bussing to abortion-on-demand.

The U.S. Constitution gives Congress the power to determine "appellate jurisdiction" of the courts. Which means that our elected officials could stop Supreme Court justices from interfering in education, or health, or anything else, simply by declaring that they had no authority to hear such cases.

In short, the House of Representatives controls the purse-strings of every federal project and program discussed in this book—and hundreds more. To put it simply, the insane spendathon in Washington will stop only when Congress demands it stop. And if the politicians presently in office won't change the policies, then it's time to change the politicians.

Members of the U.S. House are much more susceptible to voter pressure than other officials. They represent smaller districts than Senators. They come up for election every two years, not four or six. Usually, it is just a small number of informed voters who determine whether they return to Washington for another two years at the federal trough, or begin collecting their federal pension. Too often, the minority that wins is not working for lower taxes and less government; in far too many elections, the campaigning is done and the votes are delivered by various voter blocs and special-interest groups that are looking for increased subsidies and more welfare. This has got to change!

Which brings me to the final *do* in this list:

Do begin working with others who share your concerns and your hopes. The thrifty, hard-working, over-taxed citizens of this country are *not* a minority. But because the special-interest groups work together, day in and day out, two weeks before an election and two weeks after it is over, it seems as though they outnumber us. Rest assured, they don't. The problem for us Americanists has been that too many of us, for too many years, have been part of the group that watches things happen, not the activists who *make* things happen.

Well, now it's time to make a tax revolution happen!

There are thousands of local groups, hundreds of statewide organizations, and even scores of national groups working to lower taxes and reduce government. Decide for yourself which really mean business, which stand a chance of success, and which are just going through the motions. And then pitch in and support those groups that meet your approval. Support them with money; and even more important, support them with time.

Of the many groups that do exist, there are two membership groups that have already achieved national attention for their efforts.

American Tax Reduction Movement

This is the national program launched by Howard Jarvis in the aftermath of the successful passage of Proposition 13. Its objectives are very simple: to limit federal spending, and to force a reduction in taxes, *by law*.

Jarvis's American Tax Reduction Movement has proposed legislation to reduce federal spending $25 billion a year over a four-year period. Half of this reduction, or $50 billion, would go to stopping all deficits and starting to pay off the national debt. The other half would yield a twenty-percent across-the-board cut in the federal income tax, as well as reduce capital gains tax to fifteen percent. (While this last proposal has the anti-business forces screaming bloody murder, Jarvis points out that Japan and West Germany—now the two most prosperous countries in the West—have no capital gains tax at all.) Jarvis explains:

For too many years the politicians and the tax-spenders have had free reign in the halls of Congress and in our State Legislatures. The American Tax Reduction Movement will serve as a vehicle to put us, the taxpayers, back in the driver's seat.

The American Tax Reduction Movement has produced and sponsored a nationwide television program explaining its goals and inviting concerned taxpayers to join. Membership dues are $25 a year, or $100 to become a member of the National Policy Committee. The major purpose of ATRM, Jarvis explains, is to get *all* candidates for the House and Senate to take a stand on his tax-cutting proposals, and then to support those politicians who agree to work for them. The address of the ATRM is: Howard Jarvis, American Tax Reduction Movement, 6363 Wilshire Blvd., Los Angeles, California 90048.

TRIM (Tax Reform IMmediately)

The TRIM program was launched in 1974 under the slogan, "Lower Taxes Through Less Government." Committees are organized in each Congressional district; to date, more than 300 such groups have been started throughout all fifty states, making TRIM the largest, nationwide program working for tax relief.

TRIM is an official project of The John Birch Society, although it encourages persons who are not members of the Society to join. One of TRIM's primary projects is to prepare a quarterly report on key votes in the House of Representatives. The criteria used for selecting bills that appear in the *TRIM Bulletin* are: (1) Is the money appropriated over $1 billion?, (2) Is the money to be spent on wasteful and un-Constitutional programs?, and (3) Is the bill likely to have long-lasting, harmful effects on the economy if it is passed?

Unlike other national publications and organizations that rate Representative's votes, TRIM does *not* issue one survey for the country. Instead, each *Bulletin* is published within a specific Congressional district. The votes of the Representative for that district are shown, so taxpayers can tell at a glance whether he is supporting higher taxes and big government, or lower taxes and less government. Each quarterly *TRIM Bulletin* also contains short, easy-to-read articles on taxes, inflation, and the bureaucracy. As TRIM explains:

> *Many elected officials have made it a practice to tell their constituents at home one thing, while voting the opposite way in Washington. Many of them have gotten away with this deception because their votes remain buried within the pages of the* Congressional Record, *a publication that very few people read.*

Needless to say, seeing for the first time *exactly* which big-spending bills a supposedly Conservative Congressman has supported can be a shock for many voters. (And learning that thousands of copies of the record have been distributed in his district, through the *TRIM Bulletin,* can be a big shock to a Congressman!)

TRIM is an educational organization. It neither endorses nor opposes candidates for any office, federal, state, or local. Nor does it contribute to any campaign or political committee. Through literature distribution, film showings, speaking engagements, and other projects, it intends to focus attention on *issues,* not individuals:

> *TRIM's scope reaches far beyond the next election, for its purpose is not to elect or defeat candi-*

*dates, but to inform the American people.... TRIM
believes that the freedoms we have lost can only be
restored by a decrease in the size and power of
government at every level—federal, state, and
local—but especially at the federal level.*

Membership dues in a local TRIM Committee are
$24 a year, which may be paid as $2 per month. To learn
the address of the TRIM Committee for your Congressional district, contact: TRIM (Tax Reform IMmediately), 395 Concord Avenue, Belmont, Massachusetts
02178.

There are many other national organizations that
produce materials and recommend legislative action.
The Tax Foundation, the National Taxpayers Union,
and the American Legislative Exchange Council all
helped supply information and documentation for this
book.

But knowledge alone is not enough. It is time to put
all of this education to work. You must decide, *now,*
that responsible, effective action is up to you. For a
start, purchase as many copies of this book as you can
afford. Get it in the hands of your friends, neighbors,
relatives, and business associates. After all, they have
as big a stake in preserving liberty as you do.

Remember, four million Californians had a chance to
put a stop to crushing property taxes *only* because a few
thousand worked long enough and hard enough to get
Proposition 13 on the ballot.

It is up to you to prove that the Spirit of '76 is not
dead. This country was founded through a tax revolt.
And it can be saved by a taxpayers' rebellion—if you
will do your part.

Index

174 **TAX TARGET: WASHINGTON**

Other Important Books Available Through American Opinion

☐ **JIMMY CARTER/JIMMY CARTER by Gary Allen.** A shocking study of the politician with one hand on the Bible and the other behind his back — with his fingers crossed! Reveals Carter's close ties with the Rockefellers' Trilateral Commission and Council on Foreign relations. Important! Paperbound, $1.00; 10 copies, $7.50.

☐ **TEDDY BARE by Zad Rust.** The most candid and revealing account yet published of Senator Edward M. Kennedy at Chappaquiddick . . . and after. An insight into what really happened that night, and a look at those friends in high places who protected the man who may yet run for the White House. Paperbound, $2.00

☐ **THE WAR ON GOLD by Antony C. Sutton.** A definitive study of the past, present, and future of the metal that Keynesian economists have denounced as a "barbarous relic." Must reading for anyone who owns gold, or has considered purchasing some. Hardbound, $9.95.

☐ **WE HOLD THESE TRUTHS by Rep. Larry McDonald.** An inspiring study of the document that created the American Republic. Why the Constitution was written, the safeguards for freedom it established, and how it can be restored today. Deluxe paperbound, $3.95.

☐ **THE INVISIBLE GOVERNMENT by Dan Smoot.** The classic study of the Council on Foreign Relations, the elitist group that has controlled American foreign policy for over forty years. Revised and updated, with a current listing of CFR members. Large paperbound, $3.00.

☐ **NONE DARE CALL IT CONSPIRACY by Gary Allen.** With over 5 million copies in print, this runaway bestseller stunned the Establishment. Carefully documented exposé of the conspiratorial forces behind the scenes who control our government and dictate its policies. Paperbound, $1.00; 10 copies, $5.00.

Use coupon on reverse side to order books.

Order Extra Copies For Your Friends!

American Opinion
395 Concord Avenue
Belmont, Massachusetts 02178

PAPERBOUND EDITION

1-4 copies	$2.45	50-99 copies	$1.55
5-9	2.25	100-499	1.35
10-24	1.95	500-999	1.15
25-49	1.75	1000 or more	.95

Amount of Order

Tax Target: Washington	$ _____
Books from other side	$ _____
Mass. residents: add 5% sales tax	$ _____
Postage and handling	$ _____
TOTAL AMOUNT ENCLOSED	$ _____

Postage and handling charges: under $10.00 add $1.00; $10.01 to $25.00, add $1.50; $25.01 to $50.00, add $2.00; $50.01 to $100, add $2.50. Over $100.00, free.

Name _____

Address _____

City _____ State _____ Zip _____